D1591791

HELP US BEGIN

HUB strategies and mindsets for meaningful conversations with Kids, especially when you are challenged by the topic

Jen Cort, LCSW-C

Copyright © by the Association for Middle Level Education. All rights reserved. No part of this publication may be reproduced or transmitted in any form or by any means, electronic or mechanical, without permission in writing from the publisher except in the case of brief quotations embodied in reviews or articles.

Printed in the United States of America.

Citation
Cort, Jen. (2022). *Help Us Begin: HUB strategies and mindsets for meaningful conversations with kids, especially when you are challenged by the topic.* Association for Middle Level Education.

ISBN: 9781737444312

Library of Congress Control Number: 2021951870

In collaboration with Logan Cort

Contents

Part Three
Responsive HUB Mindsets and Strategies

Part Four
Advices

About the Author

Next to mom, the title I am most passionate about is a clinical social worker. I started my career with a clinical rotation in a school for students with severe mental health diagnoses. Since then, I have worked as a school counselor in elementary, middle, and high schools and am currently a high school counselor. Eventually, I became a director of student support services. Together with the counselors, nurses, learning specialists, and speech therapists, we solidified coordinated prekindergarten through the 12th-grade student support program. I assumed the role of a middle school principal and before moving on to full-time school consulting.

My motto for all aspects of my life is 'Invite the elephants in the room to tea.' The image below was a gift from my brother and artist, Charlie Pratt in 2014.

A compilation of thoughts offered by fourth-graders asked to describe what they see in the picture is, 'We can have big conversations, it may seem scary, but we are here together. And I bet there are cookies'. The motto plays on the saying 'the elephants in the room,' referring to the issues and conversations unaddressed but occupying space in our minds and relationships. We can and must engage in discussions about these complex issues, and we need to debate the complex ideas, but we need to do so while preserving our relationships. And for that, we need a particular set of skills.

It is through our relationships that we are able to hold weightier topics and have conversations about challenging matters.

About This Book

Since 2014 I have worked with hundreds of schools and organizations to redesign advisory programs to strengthen student development and build relationships between adults and kids.

The bulk of my time centers on connecting equity goals with educational practices. My job affords me the privilege of discussing complex issues around race, gender, world events, COVID-19, and more. There are countless strategies available for addressing these needs; however, they lose their impact if a community lacks the skills and capacity to process weighty topics.

Metaphorically speaking, challenging topics have heft. Without the capacity to hold the conversation, it is akin to putting heavy items in a wet paper bag. Because identity-based discussions are so important, I first focus on ensuring capacity-building skills. Building capacity is like making a bike basket strong enough to hold ponderous topics. And because our kids do better when their adults at home and school have shared language and approaches, this book is written for both parents (caregivers) and teachers to read simultaneously to have parallel or intersecting conversations.

Using This Book

Readers are encouraged to engage with this book in the way that makes most sense for their individual purposes—one section at a time or in sequence. Each section offers HUBs (Help Us Begin) mindsets and strategies for anyone who has ever been in a challenging conversation. HUBs are illustrated through stories, tips, and application methods. Many sections also have activities and workbook components.

Any one HUB mindset and strategy can support most conversations. However, here I have grouped them by proactive (thinking ahead), reactive (in the moment), and responsive (looking back to learn) strategies.

Readers might note, throughout the book, I use the term "we," which is not to presume I know how you feel or what your experiences are but rather to put us in partnership with each other. Similarly, when you read words such as "should," these are not directives. They are highlighting a topic about which I feel strongly. Finally, these offered strategies have been developed over the years, often created in response to the mistakes I have made.

Throughout the book, you will find quotes from colleagues, friends, and people whose insights into a topic have helped deepen my understanding and practice. Many of the quotes come from interviews on my podcast. To hear more of their thoughts, tune into Third Space With Jen Cort, our volunteer-fueled podcast amplifying voices as they connect to equity, diversity, inclusion, belonging, and justice.

When my children were in their last year of elementary school, I wanted a project that would give us something to focus on together and connect us during the middle school years.

Logan, my oldest, and I had a notebook that he would write in when he wanted me to know something or answer a question without talking to each other. If I saw the notebook on my pillow, I knew something was on his mind. Going back and forth, we could better unpack complicated matters with one another. We eventually extended it into a joint writing project. Our stated focus was a book on parenting middle schoolers from the perspectives of both the child and the parent. We developed a list of priorities, including decision-making, athletics, and relationships, through shared Google Docs.

Readers will meet Logan, now 21 years old, through his contributions written at 11 years old for our collaborative project. Our writing collaboration was short-lived. However, the wisdom and observations Logan offered are timeless, and I am delighted to share them with you.

I am a second child and therefore keenly aware of my own second child's experiences, always seeking to create equity between my kiddos. Therefore, the following is an insight into why you hear more of one of my children than the other. Readers will not hear our youngest kiddo's voice because our collaborative project had a different focus. Mel has always orientated around social justice. As a second-grader, Mel started a recycling program, riding a scooter around the neighborhood, picking up pounds of trash at a time. At age 11, Mel was tired of seeing injustice both in the community and in the world. My question was the same one my mother asked me throughout my life: "What will you do about it?"

Mel responded by creating Not In Our Town Olney, Brookeville, Sandy Spring,[1] or NIOTOBSS, an organization rooted in addressing inequity, bullying, and racism. My role was scheduler, driver, and most importantly, thought partner and occasional co-presenter. NIOT's inaugural event was a cross-community gathering following the 2016 election, with adults from many facets of the community engaging in discussions and activities led and designed by Mel and other middle schoolers. Mel's middle school principal, Jewel Sanders, partnered with NIOT, enriching the middle school conferences Ms. Sanders launched. NIOT has developed partnerships throughout our town and received funding to underwrite a middle school leadership program and presented at conferences calling adults into the discussion. Mel's advocacy work has continued in high school and was even featured in

---

[1] https://www.niot.org/group/niotobss

a documentary, NIOTOBSS Joins Olney Rally Against Hate Crime[2]. So, while you may not hear about Mel in this book, I am certainly proud to have collaborated and supported Mel's endeavors for equity. And I am equally proud to collaborate with Logan on this project of a different nature.

)

---

[2] NIOTOBSS Joins Olney Rally Against Hate Crime by Julie Eagle and Cheryl Crimm

Building Bicycles

Gathering your relationship-building resources

"We know, dad. You had to walk uphill both ways to school," I remember kids on a sitcom teasing their dad about exaggerating the ease of their childhood compared to his. I am among those who can genuinely say, "I walked miles to school, uphill both ways, in mud, rain, and snow." As kids, we learned to be creative in transportation around our 1,700-acre property with hills, trails, and the occasional dirt road. Distributed among our community of 1,000 people, we only had a few vehicles, and they were primarily assigned to more significant tasks, such as tilling fields or hauling and selling produce.

It was not a traditional childhood. I grew up on The Farm, now an intentional community in Summertown, Tennessee. The Farm, at the time, was a well-known and large commune. At its peak in 1979 its population grew to 1,500 members and has dwindled to about 200 today.

So, we walked to school. Both ways. No matter the weather. We also rescued horses from local dog food companies and took ponies from families who could no longer feed them. The animals were our friends, our school buses, our tractors, and more. But we had only enough horses for four or five kids to share, making them unpredictable transportation to school.

When I was around eight years old, the local bicycle factory donated (or maybe we bartered for) a truckload of bicycle parts. My friends, siblings, and I were so excited. But we couldn't just go for a ride. Farm kids learned how to do things, so we first had to build our bikes. We gathered the necessary tools and made sure we had all the correct elements in place. Under our teacher's guidance, we learned to put together gears and frames, repair tires, center the handlebars, adjust seats, and care for their upkeep. And then we rode to our heart's content, speeding around unexpected potholes or rocks in the road and experiencing the joy of flying downhill with our feet off the pedals so we could build momentum.

We even rode three kids on one little bike down a dirt road (not an activity I recommend, as I got a concussion from doing this on my ninth birthday). As with many skills learned on The Farm, bike maintenance is ingrained in me, and to this day, I know how to replace the bike chain, fix a tire, replace the brake pads, and much more.

Piece by piece, we learned to build our bikes. Help us Begin mindsets and strategies, or HUBs, are those pieces. Imagine a bicycle wheel: the center of movement comes from the wheel's hub. It holds the gears in place and creates force, allowing the wheel to turn. Imagine each wheel spoke connected to both the hub and the rim are strategies specific to that discussion. For example, a spoke might be strategies for talking about gender. Now imagine the wheel's rim is the adult and student/child relationship. Finally, the tire is the child's sense of self. As you read this book, you will gather practical tools and parts to your metaphorical bike to go on a ride with your child/student.

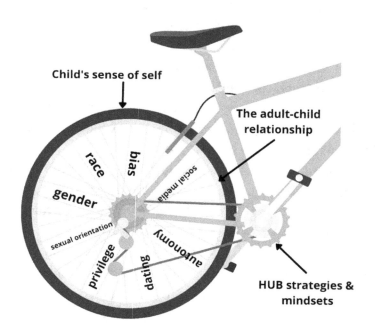

HUBs are simple yet nutrient-dense, incorporating key change model components including:

1. Recognizing a new approach may be necessary.
2. Acknowledging your roles as one who can effect change and be open to being changed.
3. Knowing your resources for support, clarification, information, and partnership.
4. Remembering we don't have to have all of the answers; we need relationships with the capacity to allow for uncertainty. Often the first and most impactful response is meaningfully asking "How *are* you?"
5. Understanding we are fallible, ever-growing people. What worked yesterday or with one kid may not the next.
6. Asking questions of yourself and others.
7. Sharing your insights, missteps, and successes.
8. Applying your new knowledge and adjusting as needed.

Part One

Proactive HUB Strategies and Mindsets

Many HUB strategies and mindsets are effective before, during, and after a challenging conversation. In this section we explore those most applicable when incorporated in advance.

1

Small Moves, Significant Impacts

Taking one step at a time to create significant changes

"Do you know what happens when you skip a stone on a pond?"

"It skips."

"And then what?"

"It ripples."

"And then what?"

"It sinks."

"And then what?"

"You pick up another stone and start again."

"And then what?"

"I don't know. What happens?"

"The bottom of the pond is forever changed because the stone is now at the bottom. And if you keep skipping stones to that same spot, the water will move differently."

I learned a lesson about creating sustainable and systemic change as I sat on the pond's edge with my then six-year-old, Logan. We'll never change the pond all at once. Yet with even one subtle movement—adding small stones to the bottom— the pond changes. We want to have dynamic and challenging conversations with our kids. But diving in too fast, like throwing a large rock in the water, can create a mess. Instead, we have to build our access points, subtly altering the foundation to prepare for, or prevent, a massive splash.

HUBs are small but impactful ideas that provide sustainable and systemic capacity-building skills that can be easily accessed and utilized. They let us form our foundation, starting small so we can build toward big. As the bottom of the pond changes with one stone, my hope is every reader will leave with one thing they will do differently.

Changing interactions and deepening relationships occur in the moments when we can think ahead and also reflect on an experience. Many HUB strategies and mindsets are effective before, during, and after a challenging conversation. In this section, we focus on proactive HUB strategies and mindsets for looking ahead. We explore those most applicable when used proactively, as part of building a strong, trusting relationship, so that a solid foundation exists when the need for difficult dialogue arises.

2

Gathering Parts and Tools

Putting *you* first

As schools moved from in-person to remote learning during COVID-19, social media posts reminding teachers and parents to take care of themselves flooded my feed. Soon after, I began seeing responses along the lines of "Anyone else realize the words 'self' and 'care' are four letters?" and "Do the people reminding us to take care of ourselves have any idea what we are dealing with?"

Self-care is complicated, I am so much better at supporting the self-care of others than of myself. It took quarantine during a global pandemic to realize how much sleep, water, time with loved ones, and laughter (and oxygen) I needed. I continue to work on it as I begin new routines that I hope will become habits. Too often, though, our well-intended self-care practices disappear, and the new, healthier habits remain unformed. Before COVID-19, I spent a lot of time on airplanes, so I have heard the *airplane rule* many times. The airplane reminds caretakers to put on your oxygen mask before assisting others, otherwise you might lose consciousness and help no one.

As you read the following section, meet the Physical Location of Feelings (PLOF), and develop a care plan, I ask you to read it twice. The first time focus only on yourself, and the second, center on the kiddos in your life.

In the video "Is Bias Useful?" author and Harvard University Psychology Professor Mahzarin Banaji observes that human survival depended partly on the idea that the people on "the other side of the mountain were dangerous. And we must get away from them." Even as humans have developed, we have kept this brain function. We experience anything other than safety, and our brains respond with fight or flight: Should I take a stand? Or should I run away?

The fight-or-flight response is entrenched in our brains, but these reactionary instincts are often negative in a modern, noncombat-oriented society. However, we can still benefit from these instincts, rerouting the process, working <u>for</u> rather than against growth. We can grow our response options by identifying and attending to the part of our body triggered by our brain. I call this part of our body the Physical Location of Feelings (PLOF).

Where PLOF resides in our bodies differs from person to person, but its functions (to protect us and remove potential harm) are consistent. Some of us know immediately what part of our body awakens when we feel stressed or vulnerable. And for many of us, identifying PLOF will take practice because we have reduced the decibels of PLOF to a nearly undetectable level.

Whether we are aware of its location or not, uninterrupted PLOF has immense power in deciding if we stay in a situation, how we treat others, and even whether we like someone. We can claim PLOF's power by acknowledging and addressing our emotions when they first begin to emerge. PLOF is like a small danger beacon in our bodies, signaling subtly at first, and then becoming increasingly loud and bright until it's screaming at us. And for many of us, PLOF is too often the decision maker.

Through a series of delicate discussions, Kay, the school nurse, connected Jeremiah's stomachaches to his anxiety over friendships. Jeremiah's visits to the nurse became less frequent as Kay and his teachers began to address the social dynamics in his class. And in so doing, they were able to help Jeremiah better his friendships and identify that his stomach was his PLOF. Through central nervous calming strategies and social empowerment activities, Jeremiah could listen to his PLOF sooner, consciously identify the environmental stressors setting him off, and take intentional actions to manage the situation. These strategies offered him self-determination, putting his brain in control and not his stomach.

We can then take care of, attend to, and soothe these PLOF reactions by identifying and listening to them at their smallest and quietest moments. The next time you feel anxious, uncomfortable, or vulnerable, ask yourself: Where do you experience it in your body? It may take a few attempts to tune into the message from the PLOF, but it gets easier with time and practice.

Like Jeremiah's (and countless other children's) stomachache, anxiety and emotional distress take up physical residences in us. Like snowflakes, our PLOF location and representation are each unique. For example, when I co-developed a mental health program with a group of seventh graders, I saw many manifestations. During one lesson, I explained the concept of PLOF and segued it into an activity to calm the central nervous system (in this case, we used mindful breathing). Afterward, students began sharing their insights, identifying how and where they experienced their emotions. Thirteen-year-old Stan listened to the lesson before declaring with frustration, "I don't know where that place is!" His foot tapped loudly on the ground and occasionally against a chair leg with increasing speed as he spoke. I asked, "If your foot could talk, what would it tell me?" His response told me everything. "It would say, I want to kick someone, but I won't because I don't want to get in trouble."

Stan unknowingly identified his foot as his PLOF, creating space to list the things he could do with his feet when they signaled discomfort. It was no surprise that he was a passionate soccer player, giving even more meaning to the value of soccer practice.

PLOF is powerful, the earlier we listen to it, the quicker we can utilize HUBs to care for our needs, disempower the reaction, and reclaim the privilege of making decisions for ourselves.

PLOF Activity One:

Identify your PLOF by recalling a stressful experience, remembering as many aspects of the experience as possible. Search your memory for your physical responses at that moment, such as stomachaches or sweaty palms. If you cannot identify it by looking back, as is the case for many of us. The next time you experience a stressor, search for your physical response. If it's difficult at the moment, then do so as soon as you. You might also ask someone you trust to observe your reactions. A friend of mine asked others to observe from their observations he learned he visibly and repeatedly clenched his teeth when he felt vulnerable.

PLOF Activity Two:

My students at Oneness-Family High School inspired this exercise for families, advisories, homerooms, and other groups. A means to write or type your responses will be helpful. Ask yourself the following questions (leaving space between sections for Step 2):

Step 1:
Think about what evokes calm, grounding, or warm fuzzy feelings. List those that you:
- See, such as a picture of a loved one, a stuffed animal, the night sky.
- Hear, such as birds chirping, children laughing, the crackling of a campfire.
- Wear or touch, such as the textures you enjoy holding or wearing. When

my children were little, we selected items from the list and called them "be braves." They could bring some of these items to school and touch them during the day if they felt nervous.

- Eat, such as the foods that bring you to another moment, reminding you of someone or introducing you to new experiences.
- Feel, such as the climate or seasons and the temperatures of foods and drinks. Be specific, for example, I love hot tea and cold tea, but only hot tea feels suitable if I'm struggling.
- Drink, such as what you might enjoy in moments of contemplation or celebration.
- Think, such as your daydreams, revisited memories, and puzzles.
- Taste includes comforting food and beverages, or specific flavor profiles like sour, sweet, bitter, or salty flavors.
- Movement, such as hugs, dance, and exercise.
- Smell, perhaps one of the strongest memory evokers, such as a favorite dessert or the perfume of a loved one.

Step 2:
Look back at your lists, circle or highlight those you have ready access to (i.e., could put in your backpack for school, have near you while working, and can easily procure). Do not circle or highlight the items that are people-, place-, or time-dependent (i.e., meaning you must be with a person, in a particular location, or at a specific time, such as a holiday.)

Step 3:
- Create two lists. List one includes the items you have ready access to, and list two includes items that are person-, place-, or time-dependent.
- Review the ready-access list. These are the resources you can use individually or in multiples to placate PLOF.

After completing the activity some families leave the lists posted inviting additions and revisions. One teacher looked at all of the lists for his advisory and created a 'care case' a box on his desk with those items shared by multiple students.

Stacy, a math teacher, delivered this activity with her advisory group. The items were fascinating and diverse, ranging from a mood ring to a photograph of a relative living in another country. Later that week Stacy noted the student wearing a mood ring and remembered it was included in her care plan as a signal of feeling uncomfortable. Recognizing this as a sign PLOF needed placating Stacy checked in with the student. The student shared that she was wearing it to help her not worry about her upcoming midterms, leading to a conversation about her anxiety and nerves. Teachers and advisors have used this activity to learn about students, create care packs (bags or boxes with needed items), and create menus for class get-togethers.

We are the caretaker of our own creativity, and we are most creative when we move with our feelings, honoring where we feel them in our bodies.

-Angie Dalton

Suggestion:
Create a *warm fuzzy* file. This is a box, pouch, or email folder to hold the messages from others that make your heart smile. Revisiting the contents of our warm fuzzy files, especially on those rough days, reminds us of who we are beyond the moment at hand.

3

PLOF Is Not a Moving Company

We can do hard things

Allured by the seduction of feeling safe and comfortable, PLOF seeks decide which conversations we will and will not participate in. One of the frequently requested topics in my workshops is about how to get people comfortable talking about the topic at hand, implying that change will not happen without everyone feeling comfortable. But it seems to me, safety should not be the goal, as growth happens in the stretch not the safe zone.

A protective PLOF

Consider the first grader proudly showing off a sweet daffodil. The flower was in a clear plastic cup, and the student pointed out the shadow of the dried dirt holding the flower in place. Squatting down to his height, I remarked on how beautiful his flower was and listened as he told that his flower, whom he names James had to work hard to push through dirt, go without frequent watering and still becoming the flower.

Like James, interpersonal growth requires some resistance, resistance balanced with care and nurturing, while partnered with the expectation of going somewhere. For many of us, PLOF confuses anything that doesn't feel comfortable, even growth, as stressful, and it attempts to get us out under the guise of protecting ourselves. Seeking and defining the stretch zones creates space for change to occur.

4

Space Patrol

When feeling safe is not the goal

In recent years, school and college campuses have created areas referred to as *safe spaces*. Many safe spaces call teachers to post trigger warnings teaching to indicate upcoming content which may be challenging or upsetting. Safe spaces intend to help students avoid traumatic situations (or situations that re-traumatize). Kids learn in every space connected to campus and what is challenging to each of us changes over time and experience, therefore the idea of safe spaces and trigger warnings as an all-encompassing protection may be quite the opposite effect leaving kids with additional vulnerability. Remaining in a safe zone is akin to going to the gym and watching other people work out. It is a way to spend your time but does not benefit your own body. It should be noted here that we are exclusively talking about intellectual safe zones. Schools should always be physically safe zones.

Michelle loved her science class. She especially loved her teacher who pushed students to ask why and challenge readily accepted answers. As they began a lesson on genetics, Michelle's teacher, Jasmine, offered trigger warning to the class outlining that some of the topics may be challenging and inviting students to tell her, take a break, or see the counselor if needed. Michelle listened to the atrocities of medical experimentation in Tuskegee and the subsequent harm caused in the name of science. Rather than being triggered by the content, Michelle found herself feeling empowered to ensure it never happened again. Affirming her decision to study science in college, she wanted to ensure these events did not occur in her lifetime. The following week, the science unit was on dissection; and since they had previously watched a dissection, there were no trigger warnings. As she put on her goggles and latex gloves, Michelle felt a deep sense of panic; her knees weakened, her breathing quickened, and she didn't know what to do. Michelle was having profound anxiety caused by the smell of latex gloves. Unexpectedly the scent took her back to her father's death in the hospital, overwhelming her with new waves of grief.

Michelle's teacher couldn't have known the smell of latex would be so triggering for her, and Michelle, not having been around gloves since his death, also did not think of them as a trigger. The teacher had intentionally created safe spaces and used trigger warnings, but still, Michelle suffered profound stress in her classroom. The school nurse called Michelle's mom, who picked her up from school and registered a complaint about the teacher, upset because the teacher knew my daughter suffered a terrible loss and believing she should have known better. Michelle's science class scenario is all too familiar; teachers have good intentions, students are still triggered, and caregivers move to protective mode.

Working together, the principal, Michelle, her mom, and Jasmine developed a new plan. The following week, Jasmine began class by co-creating classroom norms (see Intentional Norms section). These norms included focusing on self-care and activities for students to identify their PLOF. Jasmine informed the students that they should feel stretched and discomfort in her class but should not feel overwhelmed or ongoing discomfort. Adding that if students experience feelings that are bigger than they can manage in the class, they may take a drink of water, tell Jasmine, take a break, or see the counselor. Jasmine further explained that she will provide content for the class and will co-create the environment with students.

Fast forward to back-to-school night, Jasmine shared the norms with caregivers. She explained that together with students, she creates the norms and the group reviews them regularly. Jasmine asked caregivers for partnership by letting her know if their child brings a concern to you. In so doing, she established limits, empowered students, and partnered with caregivers.

Educator Tip: Reviewing norms and sharing revisions with caregivers further connects them to your goals.

In review, Jasmine:

1. Removed the trigger warnings.
2. Outlined the expectation that students should feel stretched but not sustained or overwhelmed.
3. Clarified resources (e.g., the counselor, water break).
4. Communicated with caregivers.

Jasmine's approach expanded beyond offering specific trigger warnings require teachers to know students' specific needs (even those needs elusive at the start of a term), while presuming that students' triggers are known and remain static. But there was no way for even Michelle to have known that latex gloves would overwhelm her before smelling them *during* the lesson, just like there was no way to be sure whether another lesson will upset a student or empower them.

To recap, safe zones are lovely places where we feel at ease and can relax. Safe zones are essential therapeutic areas, particularly important for folks in historically marginalized groups and dominant spaces. We need to visit safe zones regularly for restoration while not staying long. Michelle's mother wanted her to be perfectly safe in science class, but that would have robbed Michelle of the opportunity to move through her pain in a caring environment, leaving her with an unknown open wound.

Opposite the safe zone is the *stress* zone. The stress zone is where trauma, pain, and sustained discomfort take up residence. The stress zone is also not a growth zone, yet stress avoidance is both profoundly ingrained and overly simplified by societal messaging to the extent that any amount of challenge may be thought too overwhelming. Amber, arriving to class, described giving her space as traumatizing, causing a panic attach, and that she did not want to go back. Amber's hands shook and her voice was so low the teacher had to ask her to speak up to be heard and Amber nervously rushed through the presentation, sitting down without taking questions. Public speaking is scary and for some anxiety-producing. However, Amber immediately rounded up the nervous experience to traumatizing. As we later unpacked her reactions during and after the presentation, she identified nervousness, embarrassment, and feeling vulnerable but not a panic attack. With some guided self-reflection and attaching appropriate feeling words, most of Amber's feelings dissipated by the end of the day. She used her coping skills, and the next time she stood up to make a presentation, she prepared for the nerves and the vulnerability. The experience though still uncomfortable, did not repeat itself with equal intensity. It was a challenging experience, but it was not a stress zone moment.

Stress zones are like going to the gym every day, working out so much you can barely move, but still returning the next day. Stress zones are painful and may cause injury. When in a stress zone many shut down. Similarly, a brain that is continually stressed, scared, or shamed cannot grow or learn. The stress zone is just as averse to learning as the safe zone (though the impacts of the stress zone can be far more damaging). We will come back to this idea later, but it bears repeating here: **Shamed or scared brains cannot learn**.

Shamed or scared brains cannot learn.

Mike, on the other hand, was directly in the stress zone but spending his energy to convince himself he wasn't. Classmates teased Mike for his old, scuffed-up shoes and for where he lived. Mike's grades began to suffer; he started verbally acting out and shutting down in class. Mike's mom, Adele, could not elicit much from him about his experiences; her only insights came from the many calls about his behavior at school. The targeted attacks on his socioeconomic status and neighborhood produced a sustained trauma, putting Mike in the stress zone.

Adele remembered Mike's advisor invited all caregivers to be in touch at the start of the year if they felt something was amiss—an invitation the advisors repeated throughout the year. Working together, Adele, Mike, and his advisor identified the issue and raised it with the administration, who developed an appropriate response for Mike in the moment and the school as a whole.

Mike and Amber both experienced pain and discomfort. Though Amber's situation was tricky, it was also situational and quickly dissipated; therefore, it was not the stress zone. But Mike's trauma was ongoing. It stuck with him and weighed him down, producing continued, genuine stress.

In between the safe zone and the stress zone is the **stretch zone**. While working at Sidwell Friends School, I co-taught health with then PE teacher Jeff Ransom. Jeff often explained to students that muscle development depends on challenging the muscles in different ways. Like muscles, we can and should challenge ourselves to build resiliency, but not to the point of causing harm. Jeff's words on muscle development are applicable to the metaphorical muscle development for resilience, in that our growth occurs when we feel manageable to tension and stretching.

> **Like muscles, we can and should challenge ourselves to build resiliency, but not to the point of causing harm.**

Building on the work of Bobby Edwards and Rodney Glasgow, educators and diversity practitioners, we might think of a number line of 1–10. A safe zone might be a 1–2 and a stress zone a 9–10 with the ample space from 3 to 8 being the learning or stretch zone. The stretch zone is the learning zone. The goal is to be in the stretch zone as often as possible with brief visits to the safe zone for refueling. The stretch zone is like going to the gym and working out, knowing you will feel sore the next day, and knowing you can push through the soreness and be OK. The stretch zone is where growth occurs. Remembering James, the seed unable to become a flower without pushing through. The same is true of people; growth doesn't occur in a static environment without some tension, stretch, or challenge.

Once we identify our PLOF and name our zones, the process becomes conscious. We can assert our value system into the decision-making, relocating ourselves to the zone of our choosing.

Zones

Safe
Comfortable
Little to no growth

Stretch
Digging in
Growth occurs

Stress
Sustained discomfort
Little to no growth occurs

Yellow zone—— Green zone ————————————Red zone——

1 2 3   **8 9 10**

Identifying your Zones Activity:

Step 1:
Close your eyes and visualize your safe zone. How does it look, sound, and feel? If you aren't certain, imagine a place or time where you felt comfortable, at ease, or unchallenged. What, when, and/or where was that? Write your answers.

Step 2:
Close your eyes and visualize your stress zone. How does it look, sound, and feel? If you aren't certain, imagine a moment where you felt personally threatened (and again, not physically, but perhaps socially or intellectually). What, when, and/or where was that? What was said? How did you respond? Write your answers.

Step 3:
Close your eyes and visualize your stretch zone. How does it look, sound, and feel? If you aren't certain, think back to a class or teacher that inspired you,

18

that made you want to do more, or helped you better understand yourself or the world around you. Where were you? Who was the teacher? What did they do that was so impactful? Write your answers.

Step 4:
Review your answers carefully. Asking yourself:
- What do I need to move **out** of the *safe* zone?
- What do I need to move **out** of the *stress* zone?
- What do I need to **into** the stretch zone?

5

Time and Energy

How focusing on time *and* energy saves both

Have you ever read something repeatedly, not because you were unable to understand the content but because your mind drifted as you read? Or perhaps you have the necessary skills and time and spent hours on a project but didn't complete it? These are examples of expending time but *not* energy.

Syncing time *and* energy calls our attention to rethinking our relationship with both time and energy and examining the consequences of when they are out of sync. For example, when we overlay time and energy, we can spend less of both to accomplish the same we can quickly read a passage and remember the content. We can read and attend to duties more thoroughly, retain the information better, and complete the project with greater efficiency.

Our relationship with time is complex, largely negative, and reinforced in societal messaging. Consider how often the word time appears in an unfavorable context: *It's time for bed, time to go, we don't have time, I ran out of time you should have spent more time on it, and you need a time-out.*

And we do not counterbalance with positive imagery. Consider how you hear yourself (or others) say something akin to *I had the luxury of so much extra time today, there is always enough time, no rush, we have plenty of time?* These and other positive comments are not extinct from conversations, but they are rarer than the negative. Time often has an overriding presence in our lives, often determining our actions and inactions. And we pass this along to our children.

We talk to children about the time before their brains can understand it. I remember telling my infants it was time for bed, bath, or doctor's appointments. However, the brain doesn't understand the passage of time until early elementary school. This is why despite our telling them the time or date of an event, young children repeatedly ask when it will happen or how long until it does. They aren't trying to annoy us by asking over and over again, they only know that you said it would be later so asking again later makes sense. This is also why little kids often say they are three years old a few minutes later three and a half years, and so on. For the most part, they are not math wizzes but are aware they are older than they were at three years old.

A young student lamented that a friend had uninvited him from a birthday party. His teacher sought to quell his feelings. In the past, she would have said something along the lines of no to worry about it, his birthday party wasn't for months. And she would miss the mark had she done so, because the concept of months is meaningless to the child. The teacher knew that because of the children's age and developmental stage, offering and rescinding playdates and birthday invitations is one of the most powerful tools the children had. Turning attention to the child who uninvited the other, asking questions that focused on understanding what was on his mind to lead him to take back the invitation. In other words, why he was asserting power in this manner? By attending to the energy allocation for both children (and ignoring the months that would likely erase this situation from memory), the teacher could help the boys resolve the actual matter at hand.

Contrary to time, young children do understand the concept of energy. I remember finding my seat on a plane next to a mom and a toddler. The mom assured me I didn't have to worry about him disturbing me, as she showed her bag of goodies. Her purse which held snacks, drinks, diapers, new things to play with, pictures of her son's precious items at home, and lastly, a tablet accompanied by an assurance that she rarely lets him play with a tablet but would on the trip for the benefit of all. Seeing the tablet, the toddler responded with squeals of delight, motioning that he wanted to play, and showing no interest in any other item in the magic bag. However, he could not turn it on. In her hurry, the mom forgot to charge the tablet. Though not entirely verbal, he had watched his mom often model how to charge a tablet. On the edge of a meltdown, the toddler mimicked plugging in the device through gestures. While he couldn't comprehend the word (energy) or how the tablet worked, he understood that the way to get the tablet to work was by plugging it in. Luckily, I had a backup charger to lend and the child immediately set to plug into the tablet.

In late elementary and early middle school, many teachers and caregivers focus on managing time with planners, calendars, and more. Learning to allocate enough time for the task at hand is an essential skill. So too is knowing how to intentionally apply the necessary energy to accomplish the task. Both time and energy are limited in quantity. **The earlier we teach children to consciously allocate their energy, the better they will use their time.**

Greg loudly entered our Diversity Leadership Workshop, landing his backpack with a loud thump, and grumbling that he studied so long and could not fail a test. Another student asked Greg, if he had spent so much time? Energy? Or both. He had spent *time*, but his mind and energy were on an argument he had with his crush. Greg worked with the school counselor to help him develop strategies for handling disagreements and better optimize his study time and grades.

> **The earlier we teach children to consciously allocate their energy, the better they will use their time.**

Many of us have to *unlearn* habits, aligning time and energy takes effort. However, the process gets easier with practice. We start by differentiating between time and energy. Time management is prioritizing tasks, allocating time needed for assignments, and ensuring the completion of necessary items. We accept that time and energy may go hand in hand yet are not synonymous. Energy allocation is focusing on what is necessary to reducing energy consumers while reclaiming our focus to the task at hand.

Help Us Begin

Working on time and energy, I asked middle schoolers to listen for words or phrases exemplifying both. Time prompts included listing the things to do before bed, discussing the schedule, counting down to an event (five minutes, two minutes), asking questions 'such as what do you have to do today?' and using words such as 'it's time to go!' One student shared, when upset, his mom may not talk a lot but her voice changes and she repeats herself, both of which make him nervous. Energy prompts were fewer and more challenging to identify. Energy comments included teachers asking students asked what they needed. One student offered that he thought his grandmother helped him find energy by giving him a hug as soon as he got home and then giving him quiet to relax after school.

We know if we fritter away our time, it is gone, and we cannot make more of it. The same is true of energy. When explaining energy allocation to students, I use a pizza metaphor. If we have a pizza and I eat a slice, it is gone. We can't will another piece to appear. So, when an experience or emotions consumes our energy, that energy has to be taken from something else. Therefore, by thinking about time management and energy allocation in combination as a mutually informing process, we can spend less of each.

Most of us have experiences or parts of ourselves that require more energy than others. One immense energy consumer is code-switching. Code-switching is contorting oneself to fit into an environment such as adjusting language, hair, accent, clothes, talking about who they love and more. This process means those who have to code-switch are walking in the door with less energy available to accomplish the same tasks. Des, a 7th grader shared that she is the only Black girl in her grade and code-switches all the time by changing her hair, clothing, and more. Des described leaving home feeling her full self (63 inches tall) and by the time she arrives at school she feels closer to 60 inches. Throughout the day (depending on the teachers, students, and curriculum) her experience of her metaphorical height fluctuates but is never all of her and is often half. Des, a student at a predominantly White school, code-switches throughout the day to fit in, therefore can't show up as her full and authentic self.

Teachers in another school work with students to identify the factors depleting and restoring their energy. A sixth grader, the only person in his school wearing a hearing aid and feared being teased. He spent years fixing his hair such that much of the hearing aid was covered. In a discussion about energy, he shared, that doing so felt like running with a heavy backpack to make it to the school door at the same times as those without the additional weight. The student reminds us of the importance of identifying the energy we expend on unexpected challenges, distractions, and code-switching.

Tip: When debriefing or reviewing experiences, separate time from energy asking how both were consumed and reclaimed.

6

Norms Happen

Creating *intentional* norms

Norms are patterns of behavior identifying how we expect (or are expected) to exist. While norms exist in all settings, they are often *unintentional* rather than *intentional*. Unintentional norms may be sitting at the same desk in the classroom or chair at the dinner table, even though there are no assigned seats. Intentional norms are assigned. Intentional norms provide routines, agreements, consistency, and a framework to address complex situations. Imagine norms as the container holding a delicious soup. The soup has many beautiful ingredients, but the components would spill all over the counter and make a mess without the container. When norms are intentionally created, and particularly when created with equal input from students and adults, they provide the container, or context, in which young people and adults can work together in a classroom or home.

Intentional norms are an essential role in creating the ethos of the classroom, home or other gathering, and are permanently attached to and informed by our values. A ninth grader offered that closing the bathroom door is an unintentional norm, explaining, no one polices closing the door, but we all do it. Students also said that talking to friends between classes, carrying books for two classes in a row so they don't have to return to lockers and changing for PE in the same spot every day are all examples of unintentional norms.

Turning attention to intentional norms another student, expanded on the previous bathroom metaphor offering an example that his family has a small water heater and is committed to being environmentally conscious, therefore they all take five-minute showers. The family had discussed water consumption and developed a set of norms to meet their goals. Lastly, the teacher connected putting homework in the basket upon first arriving to class as an intentional norm she created.

The identification of intentional and unintentional norms creates opportunities for change. By looking at how behavior moves around and within these norms, we are better able to develop patterns directly relating to our values.

CLARIFYING AND COMMUNICATING VALUES

Mike enthusiastically stated his family values soccer. As we dug deeper, we found that Mike's family truly loves soccer but values being a good team member, learning to win and lose well, and being physically active. Soccer in this case, is the conveyance or method of expressing those values, but soccer, in and of itself, is not a value.

Mike's confusion (the activity vs. the values) is common for people and for schools. I often hear a range of responses, from vague, need-to-be-defined ideas such as *community* (which can have numerous and varied interpretations), to specific activities or experiences, such as soccer. Therefore, clarifying values first before creating intentional norms, grounds the norms in the values.

Our values reflect our hearts. They articulate and inform who we are, and what we stand for and what we stand against. Values give meaning to relationships, adding reflection points in challenges, and inform every aspect of our lives. Values are internal with subtle shifts throughout our lives. They are the essence who we *are*, not what we *do*.

Our beliefs or practices might change as we learn more about ourselves and how we stand in the world. Years after a difficult divorce, Carol reflected that she used to believe marriage, even an unhealthy one, was forever; a belief that changed as her marriage disintegrated. But what did not change was her value of meaningful, loving, committed relationships. Carol's belief (marriage is forever) and conveyance (commitment to her partner) shifted, but her values (meaningful and loving relationships) were clarified by her experiences while remaining essentially the same.

Values are taught in small moments and experiences over time. We can't simply pour our values into kids. We share, talk, and lecture, while our kids listen and observe. As they learn from our actions, words, and inactions, kids' values will form and clarify as they have their own experiences. Kids look for our consistency of our action's relation to our value, such that even when we have not verbalized the value, kids connect to them through our modeling.

On The Farm we had Sunday Service every week. It was a gathering time to meditate as a community, learn more about events in the outside world, and hear our community's reactions to those events (demonstrating the community's values). Full disclosure: I wasn't the most attentive person in Sunday Service. I loved the warm weeks when we all sat in the meadow, but I was far more engaged in adding houses and roads to my secret fairyland than I was in the messages shared during the service. Truth is, if asked as a child, I probably would have said Sunday service was boring.

When I was in eleventh grade, my family left The Farm and moved to Oyster Bay, Long Island. To my tremendous surprise, I found myself yearning for the Sunday Service that was now a thousand miles and another lifetime away. I began visiting places of worship with my friends, and later in college, on my own, trying to find a similar experience of reflection and faith. In bringing me to Sunday Service throughout my childhood, my parents imbued in me a desire to be a part of a community, an understanding that I was part of a bigger picture, and the need for a central force around which to orient myself. These were my values. So, with my girlfriends, I attended Catholic Mass, Shabbat with my boyfriend and found other places of worship on my own. I sought the conveyance (going to a shared, faith-based gathering) of my values. My search continued until my early 20s when I was the counselor at Sidwell Friends School, a Quaker School. In our new employee orientation, our Head of School, Earl Harrison, shared that Quakerism held many of the same values as other faiths including peaceful conflict resolution, the belief in the good of all, and equity. He explained that some of us may find the experience of being in a Quaker school as a validation of our beliefs in other religions, for some it may be a time for quiet, and for others we find Quakerism feels like home. I found myself in the latter group.

Conflating conveyance (soccer, Sunday services, etc.) with values (e.g., being a team member, belief in being part of something bigger than oneself) is an easy pattern to fall into. Clarifying values at home, and school provides a frame of reference for all.

Example values and conveyances:

	Value	Conveyance (means by which value is taught or lived out)	Demonstration of value
Home	Being kind	Teaching kids to resolve conflicts thoughtfully.	Arguments and disagreements are resolved respectfully.
School	Arriving ready to learn	1. Regularly reviewing what materials are needed for class. 2. Teaching social and emotional skills to resolve matters. 3. Starting class with activities to calm the central nervous system.	1. Students show up with relevant materials. 2. Students learn incrementally to clear the mind of distractions and focus on task at hand.
Home	Contributing to the family	Assigning chores and ensuring kids know how to complete them.	The family holds meetings to revise chores and to hear thoughts and opinions of all.

Clarifying Values Activity for Home and School (for Adults and Kids):

Values Clarification, Part 1:

1. Allow your mind to wander and list everything important to you, such as feelings, experiences, people, things, and opportunities.
2. Review the list.
3. With 30 seconds to a minute for emergent readers, cross off:
    a. Repetitive items (e.g., cross off *swimming* if you've already listed *sports*).
    b. Things.
    c. Activities and accomplishments. (Identify the driving force behind activities and achievements.)
    d. At the end of the process, you should have a few values left on the list.
4. Look at your list. Do you notice patterns?
5. Write a description of yourself using your values, and provide examples (e.g., I value doing my best, such as when I put six hours into my history presentation).
    a. Ask the group to close their eyes or cast them aside. (*Note: The option of casting aside is offered because we don't know who has suffered trauma and closing eyes in front of others may be restimulating.*)
    b. Imagine you are going into a large room filled with people. Everyone in the room has a list of names and descriptions of each person's values separately. The task is to match the values with the person. What needs to be on your list so that people could identify you?
    c. Review your description of yourself and revise as necessary.
6. In the classroom or at home, you might post the values in a visible spot and do a "gallery walk," reading each other's list without comment.

Values Clarification, Part 2:

1. Gather the class or family together to determine the group's values following steps 1–4 above.

2. Post them in a visible spot and encourage the group to add to them over time.

3. Hold a meeting to develop a *values statement*. For example, "Our family holds our relationships with each other as central to our values. We value talking across differences, listening for learning, and know we can do hard things."

Taking a step further:

You might ask the group for each value to list accompanying belief(s) and conveyance(s). For example, standing up for and with others is one of Anna's values. And the conveyance of this value is through advocacy work.

INTENTIONAL NORMS

Identifying our values, quickens the development of intentional norms. Many teachers and advisors develop norms at transition points such as the beginning of the year, term, or quarter. Intentional norms rest upon our values and inform behaviors. For example, in a classroom, that might be to arrive for to class with the necessary materials. This norm builds on the value of showing up ready to learn and the expected behavior is for students is to arrive to class with all the necessary items. In a family, a norm might be not having devices at the table. This norm builds on the value of being fully present in the family, and the expected behavior is leaving phones in a separate room or stack them together at a side table before dinner.

Steps for Creating Intentional Norms

Part 1: Build your list of norms

1. Questions for adults or leaders to consider prior to engaging in a discussion:
   a. What are the values I want the norm to support?
   b. How will (or how have I) I communicate(d) the values?

c. How will the kids' voices be invited into and heard in the discussion?

d. Where are the areas in which I can be flexible?

2. Outline the goals, answering *why* intentional norms are essential to you and for the group.

3. Focus first on the values and then the habits or conveyances.

4. Include all voices, giving think time and outlining the expectations of the discussion.

5. Communicate boundaries. As the adult in the discussion, it is helpful to draw boundaries at the onset of the debate. For example, Kim was leading her class through a norm's articulation activity. One of the classes values is to acknowledge and celebrate hard work. Knowing her class would ask for but could not have a party every day, Kim offered that celebrating hard work is important, they would have a party once per quarter, and inviting the class to think about everyday ways to celebrate. By drawing the limit around having a class party once a month, Kim opened the discussion for other ideas. A family wanting to do something different but having a tight budget might tell the children they have time on Saturday afternoon, a budget of $20, and be offered a list of activities from which to choose.

Part 2: Living with (and testing) the list

A challenge plan is perhaps the most important, and easily overlooked, part of intentional norm planning. Norms, no matter how they are developed or how good they are, will be tested and testing is often interpreted as disrespect or lack of caring. Preparing a challenge plan asks of the group how they respond when the norm is tested or breeched reduces feeling off guard and better prepares the group. Developing new habits and patterns takes time and practice and is often uneven. If a pattern emerges with one or two people testing norms frequently, it may be a behavioral matter best served with a direct discussion. On the other hand, if the *group* struggles, it is likely the norm that needs recalibrating.

Part 3: Communication

Educators might communicate your norms to other teachers of your students and to. Caregivers might also wish to tell homeroom teachers or advisors about family agreements and values.

Communication between home and school presents an opportunity to share home and school culture and traditions. Bonus! Information about our processes also helps to reduce loyalty conflicts. Alex, an English teacher, writes a letter to her students and caregivers over the summer. In the letter sharing her goals and why her classroom norms are essential. She includes an invitation for families to share their culture, values, and challenges as a means to learn about her students and communicate her partnership with families. This outreach connects her with students and invites partnership with caregivers.

Part 4: Checking in

Understanding that norms are not static, it is helpful to review and revise them regularly. Group prompts for revising norms include:

1. Is this norm working?
2. Does this norm help us live out our values?
3. Are there other strategies we might use?
4. How would you describe this norm in your own words?

Co-constructing (students and adults working together) norms is not about memorizing a list of rules repeated on cue. It is about creating a framework, of shared understandings for how the group interacts with each other. Stating them in our own words supports this goal.

For example:

Rules for settling into class demonstrate compliance and may encourage students to nonverbally communicate rather than being ready to learn.

1. Walk in quietly.
2. Put homework in bin on teacher's desk.
3. Sit down.
4. Have materials for class.

Intentional norms for arriving to class ready to learn, allowing for a minute to greet friends, and demonstrating readiness to learn by having necessary materials.

1. Take a minute to settle into your desk.
2. Demonstrate being ready to learn.

Intentional norms are fewer in number and are developed with, and on behalf of the group. I knew a teacher who noticed students needed more movement and invited her math students to sit at a desk or on a yoga ball. The choice was up to the students long for as they demonstrated readiness to learn. The norms were sit in the best place for you and demonstrate readiness to learn.

The saying 'less is more' is particularly applicable to norms. Too many norms mean some will be forgotten. Similarly, when norms are vague, such as 'be respectful,' they are ripe for misinterpretation as words like respect differ across ages, cultures, and more. Intentional norm construction asks, 'What does this norm look and sound like?' and 'How will we know if the norm is not working?' When creating intentional norms, it is helpful to ask the group to consider what might be missing from the list. If your group has a long list of norms, you may want to put them aside for a later discussion, focusing on combining and collapsing them.

Clarifying values and establishing norms reduces confusion, builds community, engages all voices, and deepens capacity for growing through challenges.

Educator Activity: Creating Intentional Norms

1. Outline the goals and benefits of norms.
2. Connect all norms to values (noting classroom practices not connected to values are probably habits rather than norms and may be unnecessary).
3. Include the student voice, giving think time, outlining the expectations of the discussion, and allowing personal concerns to be raised outside of the group discussion.
4. Communicate boundaries and expectations. Many folks are frustrated when we believe we are working as a group to generate ideas and the

facilitator has not communicated intended outcomes or ideas that are not optional areas before the discussion.

5. Ensure inclusion for how norms for how the group will respond when the norms are challenged.
6. Review and revise regularly.
7. Communicate the norms with students and caregivers.

7

When You Think I Saw or Heard and You Did Not See or Hear Me Respond

Kids and adults in partnership to address issues as they arise

Living in the DMV (DC, Maryland, Virginia) area, our Pre-K and Kindergarten teachers invited students from Gallaudet University[1] to work as teaching interns. Gallaudet University is a school for deaf or hard-of-hearing students. The interns from Gallaudet taught our Sandy Spring Friends School[2] students and teachers several signs that allowed for quick, nonverbal communication in the classroom. 'I see you' became on one of the signs we incorporated, becoming so ingrained in our school culture that it moved from elementary to middle school for at least one student.

The signal connected us. But I made a tremendous mistake and caused harm when I relied on it without inviting students to communicate concerns. One day, as I entered the eighth-grade pod, a cluster of classrooms and lockers, I noticed some students standing in a tight group at the end of the hall. I sensed the energy was off but didn't know why. *Mike* saw me and quickly signed the check-in sign. I

---

[1] Gallaudet University, a local university for deaf and hard of hearing
[2] Sandy Spring Friends School, a Kindergarten through twelfth-grade independent school

returned the sign and reminded the students that the bell had rung. Feeling unsettled, I peeked into the classroom and saw Mike's head bent over his work, seemingly nothing was amiss. I continued with the morning. When I saw Mike in the cafeteria, I inquired how he was, heard he was ok, which I interpreted it to mean everything was good, told him I was glad and headed to a meeting.

When I arrived at school the following day, I saw Mike and his mom outside my office, visibly unhappy. Once in my office, Mike's mom passionately explained that when in the hall, Mike had a racist comment made to him, noting I was present and did nothing. She further shared that when I saw him in the cafeteria, I asked, in front of others, if he was alright before quickly leaving for a meeting. Everything Mike's mom described was true. I was there, I did see him, he knew I saw him, and I did ask him in front of other kids if he was OK. And because I asked him in front of others, it would have been tough to say anything other than 'yes'. And I did rush off to my meeting and doubt I gave it another thought.

Mike's mom continued, telling me I had failed our middle school motto, "Thriving not surviving middle school." The motto reflected the faculty and staff intentions to ensure my students have a physically, emotionally, academically, and socially safe environment. On that day for Mike, and I am sure for others, I had not lived out our motto.

To address the gap between thriving and surviving, I needed to address the racist comment and develop strategies to prevent a recurrence. I also needed to adjust my behavior, leading to the creation of a partnership question: 'If you think I saw or heard and you didn't hear or see me respond, I would like you to...' The person asking the question provides multiple responses such as to tell me, email, tell another (asking them to tell me) and so on.

This tool helps create partnership and provides accountability. Sometimes we see or hear problematic statements or actions and don't respond because we don't have time, aren't sure how to, or hope someone else will. Sometimes we don't respond to events because we didn't hear or see what happened. And we may see or hear something, but it did not have equal impact to us as it did for our students. Using the sentence stem 'If you think I saw or heard...' has helped me countless times and I wish I had it prior to that moment with Mike.

An example of this strategy in action is 'If you think I saw or heard but didn't see or hear me respond, I ask you to tell me in person, with a friend, or by email. And if for any reason that doesn't feel right, I invite you to tell (fill in the blank with other adult names). As always, you are welcome to talk to me with a friend or adult ally present. You should be supported so please don't let it go until you feel settled and/or heard.'

Let's look more closely at the goals for each part of the message above.

Section:

"If you think I saw or heard but didn't see or hear me respond, I ask you to tell me in person or by email."

Goals:

1. Communicate my awareness that I will not always get what is impactful to my students.
2. Provide discussion options for communicating with me.

Section:

"And if for any reason that doesn't feel right, I invite you to tell (fill in the blank with other adult names)."

Goals:

1. Acknowledge that what feels right to one may not to another.
2. Ensure students know they can communicate concerns directly with other adults or with me.
3. Invite approaching another adult al~~~~ ~~~~ feel uncomfortable approaching me

Section:

"As always, you are welcome to talk to ~~~~

Goals:

1. Focus on the student's needs rather ~~~~
2. Create expectation of being suppor~~~~

[handwritten note on attached paper:]
↳ open/honest communication can look and sound different, but should always occur

↳ getting on the "same page"

Section:

"No matter your choice, please don't let it go until you feel settled and/or heard."

Goals:

1. Avoid asking, "Why didn't you tell me?"
2. Create for the student the expectation of being heard, which should be true of all experiences. But we know some victims of abuse report telling someone, and if nothing happened, they may not tell anyone else.
3. Outline expectations for my accountability to students.

Child–Adult Partnership Reflection Activity:

1. Imagine a child experiencing distress and believe you saw or heard the cause. Would you like the child to tell you what happened? If so, answer the following:
   a. What if they did not feel comfortable telling me?
      i. Are there others they could tell? If so, who?
      ii. Can the conversation be in person only? If not, what are other avenues of communication? (Teachers, please check your school's communication policies.)
   b. What would you hope the child would do if they told you but didn't feel heard by you?
   c. Is it OK to bring someone into the conversation?
   d. In what ways can we invite accountability?
2. Look at your answers to the questions and finish the sentence "If you think I saw or heard and didn't see or hear me respond, I ask you to...."
3. Practice saying it aloud.

Part Two

Reactive HUB Strategies and Mindsets

Part Two focuses on reactive strategies that are to be accessed in the moment. Reactive strategies ask questions, seek clarification, and establish check-ins for following up.

8

Once You Learn, You Will Always Know How to Ride a Bike

Understanding, naming, and managing neurological shortcuts

The saying 'once you learn to ride a bike, you will never have to learn again' is often true. I learned of Scott Barry Kaufman, a cognitive scientist and humanistic psychologist,[1] while watching the show Brain Games.[2] Kaufman asserts that our brains have a system of categorization and in each category is an optimal example to be most quickly accessed. I think of these as *neurological shortcuts*. For example, when learning to ride a bike, our bodies are taught how to hold balance and push the pedals. Our brain remembers and communicates the steps to our bodies. Learning to ride a bike is creating a new *neurological shortcut* for ourselves, which we access every successive time we hop on the bike.

Designed for efficiency, we all have and need many of our neurological shortcuts. Shortcuts allow learned information and experiences to become fixed. For most, learning to tie shoes was, at first, an uphill task, so much so, teachers

---

[1] https://scottbarrykaufman.com/bio/
[2] https://www.youtube.com/watch?v=QelK8rDrbpM

of young children often include shoe-tying time in their transition planning. However, once known, shoe tying becomes automatic, allowing us to do so without so much as looking at our shoes. Another example is arriving somewhere you regularly travel without considering your route; throw a detour in which you do not have a shortcut, and suddenly you must put your primary focus on the route.

Our neurological shortcuts are essential for functioning in everyday life. Imagine how long it would take us to get dressed if every day we had to learn each step as we put on our pants, brush our teeth, or zip our jackets. So strong is our brain's desire for an answer or response, our shortcuts can also develop from the absence of experience or knowledge and because they are designed for efficiency, our shortcuts may take snippets of information and create a response to even complex situations. Shortcuts are not informed by values, moral code, personal ethics, or even the accuracy of information. Our brain does not, for example, stop us to ask our values about how we tie our shoes or our ethics around brushing our teeth. Therefore, despite their essential roles in our lives, our shortcuts can lead us down unhelpful paths.

When Logan was 14 and a recently certified scuba diver, he had the privilege and opportunity to scuba dive in an aquarium. Wanting to explore and exert his independence, he questioned me about why I was walking with him to the dive spot. As his mom, there was no question, and I was grateful that the requirement to sign release forms became the perfect cover for accompanying him. Knowing nothing about diving except that my kiddo loved it, I listened carefully as the instructor spoke about his years of diving, certifications, and more. Because my neurological shortcuts of credibility include longevity in the field, education, and awards in the space of a few moments, my neurological shortcuts told me the dive instructor was qualified, and I trusted him to take my *baby* into a massive aquarium.

When invited to ask questions, I asked perfunctory questions about safety concerns and the pick-up time. Finally, I wonder aloud how the dive instructor would ensure my son avoiding the sharks in the big tank, asking instead if he could swim with the dolphins. Our son doesn't often verbally express his annoyance with me, but sometimes his silence is loud enough to feel like he is screaming. This was one of those moments. Taking a deep breath, the dive instructor told me I should *never* allow your son to swim with dolphins in an enclosed tank. Further that I should *only* allow your son to swim in a tank with sharks. Instantly, my newly found confidence in his qualifications disappeared. The instructor's extensive experience meant nothing to me. Again, with no diving knowledge, so strong were my shortcuts about sharks and dolphins, I determined that he was wrong, and began thinking of a plan to get my son out of the situation.

But the dive instructor took the time to explain that dolphins are largely muscular and even when in small environments they will establish high rates of speed. He also explained that dolphins, out of pure curiosity, may smash Logan against the clear glass windows. Sharks, however, are largely skeletal, swimming at lower speed and in a snakelike motion. They're not curious about people unless they're hungry and confuse fingers for food. He assured me the sharks were well-fed and divers were advised to keep their fingers flat by their bodies as a precaution. Finally, the instructor advised that if Logan stays out of the shark's way, they will stay out of his. Because of his explanation, like a boomerang, a new shortcut was created and I was again convinced to let Logan dive and now had new shortcuts about sharks and dolphins.

Unchecked, our shortcuts become our biases and actions. In this case, the dive instructor took the time to explain and therefore undo my previous shortcut. However, often we do not have the time or desire to have our thought changed, making it all the more important for us to recognize our shortcuts. Through education and experience, we can reroute them.

So why did someone with no diving experience decide the diver was, and then was not, competent to take my child into the water? Let's examine how quickly my shortcuts decided for me:

1. I was nervous about my son diving in an aquarium. My PLOF was awake and ready to determine my actions. (See the section on The Physical Location of Feelings or PLOF).

2. I determined through the media messages (and no direct experience) that sharks were scary and would eat you, and that dolphins were friendly and cute.
3. Hearing his years of experience, the number of dives, and places worked, I believed the dive instructor to be credible and competent.
4. I heard information inconsistent with my shortcuts (swim with sharks!) and immediately switched my determination of the dive instructor, deciding he was incompetent and untrustworthy.

My determinations happened quickly and subconsciously, leading me to a *truth* about the instructor without engaging my value system or my ethics. Thankfully, the dive instructor recognized my lack of information and took the time to educate me (as I'm sure he's done for countless previous caregivers). He rerouted my short-cuts. As I watched from outside the aquarium, I saw our son enjoying every minute of the dive, playing rock, scissors, paper with young kids on the other side of the glass and I watched sharks move out of his way.

When we are unfamiliar or less familiar with a situation, we often build whole narratives out of snippets of information and respond according to that created narrative. For example, my youngest child once proclaimed, a distaste for eating nuts despite never having had nuts before. But Mel's internal narrative about nuts was built on the knowledge that my husband is highly allergic. Our shortcuts cause us to leap into a presumed understanding that we have not come to genuinely. While an aversion to the food you've never tried is a relatively harmless example, other shortcuts can be far more complex and damaging, such as treating a group of people negatively because of the media, other people's biases, or our history with a single individual. And sadly, the onus of rerouting our shortcuts is often placed on the person on the other end of our shortcut (like the dive instructor), tasking them with informing and educating us.

The responsibility of rerouting our shortcuts is our responsibility, and we all have the power to quickly and meaningfully dispatch our shortcuts. The plasticity of our brains allows us to incorporate new information quickly, and when cen-tered on our values, we can create sustained change. Once we learn to ride a bike, we don't unlearn how to do so. But if we encounter a new type of bike, sustain an injury, or our body type changes, we can reset, adjust, untangle the old skill and build a new, more appropriate one. By asking ourselves how our shortcuts inform our experiences and treatment of other we can better reroute our short-cuts before they become our biases and stereotypes. For example, some readers may now have a new shortcut about sharks, dolphins, and diving because of newly received information.

The formula for rerouting shortcuts is to:

1. Ask yourself *why* you responded as you did.
2. Connect to your values.
3. Determine the education or experience you need to reroute the shortcut.
4. Gather your resources.
5. Create a response plan.

How we reroute our shortcuts is unique to each person. Still, there are some con-sistent practices we can all implement, such as backward examination, reflecting on values, asking questions, engaging in mindfulness practices, and listening to PLOF. See also the Communicating Values and PLOF Is Not a Moving Company sections.

The backward examination is the practice of asking, "Before I believed this, what did I believe?" For example, before I became a Quaker, I believed Quakers were Amish. Before I believed Quakers were Amish, I believed Quakers didn't use electricity. Before I thought Quakers didn't use electricity, I thought Quakers were of the past. Continuing with this process, I realize I had not known about Quakers; therefore, I had shortcuts about their faith. I could not imagine becoming Quaker before I worked at Sidwell Frier ~~~~ School. But working ~~~~ new information, experiences, and opportu ~~~~ imagine *not* being a Quaker.

Backward examination is suppor ~~~~ activities to calm the central nervou ~~~~ including meditation, intentional bre ~~~~ backward examination we are better ~~~~ our shortcuts.

[handwritten annotations:]

↳ avoiding stereotypes and biases

"re-routing"

↳ build narratives that encompass all info, not just snippets

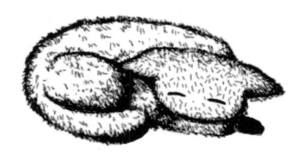

A settled PLOF

Tips:
1. Ask yourself what are your metaphorical sharks and my dolphins?
2. Practice slowing down your responses, allowing for *think time.*
3. Assert power over your PLOF.
4. Use backward examination questions when you have a quick reaction, particularly about an individual or groups of people.

9

Use One Sentence

Use fewer, more impactful words in challenging situations

When we are stressed, anxious, or our PLOF seeks to assert control, and we tend toward extremes. In those moments we may verbally either go on and on filling the space with words or using fewer words than necessary for healthy communication.

An activated PLOF

Dan knew he had to have a difficult conversation with his son, Josh, after hearing about Josh's disruptive behavior in school. Dan was nervous and felt underprepared for the discussion, leading to his words tumbling out like a dam flooding over.

Josh sat still, nodding at times but also counting the ceiling tiles. Later describing that he simply had to check out because his dad kept on talking. The next day

Dan shared with friends that he and Josh had a serious discussion, and Josh now understood how to act. Josh did not share this view as he was annoyed that his dad talked so long, he missed a level on his video game. Dan indeed stated his concerns, but they did not hold the same meaning for Josh because the overwhelming number of words drowned out the actual message.

Angela and her mom have the opposite dynamic, handling challenging topics with silence. Angela's mom received an email from the school about a sexist comment made to Angela and she wanted think time before talking with her daughter. Angela knew the teacher had called and suspected the conversation was coming but didn't know when or where. Her mom's silence was longer than usual, making hours feel like days, leading Angela to conclude her mom was angry with her. The anxiety and anticipation made it difficult for Angela to study for her test, compounding an already difficult situation with increased (and unnecessary) academic pressure.

We can avoid word vomit or loud silence by giving ourselves a structure to work within such as the *One-Sentence Response*. One-sentence response prompts us to make the sentence *nutrient dense*, packed with meaning in the message. One sentence also calls us to pause and listen before speaking again. Note, the one sentence is not a run on and works when it is a legitimate sentence with a start, middle, end. We then speak with one sentence at a time, allowing space for response. Having heard the other person, we offer another sentence, continuing until the conversation concludes.

For Dan, using the one-sentence strategy might sound like:

Dan: Josh, can we talk either before or after dinner about your perspective on what happened in school today? (*Co-scheduling, allowing Josh choice, previewing the topic for Josh.*)

Josh: I guess before dinner.

Dan: Thank you. And where would you like to meet?

Josh: My room.

Before dinner, in Josh's room:

Dan: I brought a glass of water and a snack (care of PLOF). I want to hear how you experienced the day, particularly English class. (*Open-ended invitation to share while guiding Josh to English class.*)

Josh: He wouldn't call on me, so I told my friends what I wanted to say.

Dan: Can you tell me what you wanted to share in class?

Josh: *Tells his dad what he wanted the teacher to hear.*

Dan: Thank you for sharing that. I wish he had heard your thoughts, too. Could we work together on some strategies to avoid a repeat of this situation?

Dan and Josh's next step would be to create a *menu of strategies*. The menu might offer options such as moving seats toward the front of the room, writing down what he wanted to share, or talking to the teacher. Menus have realistic boundaries and avoid unfeasible ideas, such as "firing the teacher" (more on creating menus below). Josh reviewed the menu and decided which strategy to try first. Dan, sensing they are at the end, scheduled a follow-up meeting.

Educator using one sentence:

English teacher, Alice reviewing the chapter of the book assigned over the weekend. A student comments to a classmate (in a voice loud enough to be heard by Alice and most of the class) with a pivot topic asking why the class was discussing Shakespeare instead of the graffiti appearing on the temple over the weekend.

Alice: Elli, I hear you and we need to discuss it, let's finish this one piece, and then we can discuss.

Elli: I tried to talk about it in math, b

Alice: I don't know that I can help eith soon as we review the scene.

In the above example, Alice needed a one sentence at a time. Alice acknowled around the timing, thus giving herself a fe

10

Limit Use of Diagnostic Words

Use mental health words in mental health situations and feeling words in all others

Sorry I was late. I had an ADD moment.

This weekend, I was a little OCD. I organized my entire room!

After watching that movie, I had a complete panic attack.

These statements are examples of students using mental health diagnostic words to describe regular, daily events. ADD (attention deficit disorder), OCD (obsessive-compulsive disorder), and panic attacks are diagnoses made by qualified professionals to describe a cluster of ongoing symptoms. After checking with the students, we learned one was having difficulty paying attention to the task at hand. Another student felt better after organizing her room. The last student watched the movie and was spooked. None of them had ADD, OCD, or experienced a panic attack.

The merging of diagnostic words into our vocabulary has become a way we describe *big* feelings. It is a merger with a high risk of negative consequences. As one student offered that when people say they had an ADD moment, she wanted to scream adding that ADD it isn't a moment. Finally, that ADD It is ongoing, requires accommodations, taking medicine, and meetings with the learning specialist.

Mental health and neurological diagnoses have multiple criteria and a diverse set of ranges. Therefore, even when someone has a diagnosis, the label (ADD) neither informs how one experiences the criteria nor explains what responses might be helpful.

A colleague once wondered if our students' increased casual use of diagnostic terms reflected their desire to destigmatize mental health matters giving me something to puzzle over. To be sure, we need to destigmatize mental health and expand support for mental health care through accurate diagnostics, access to, and affordability of, mental health care. And students consistently report mental health as lacking or absent in their education with many describing it as the identifier that is both the least understood and most often stigmatized.

Students often request adults initiate conversations about mental health, noting, that even when we don't know how to respond, they still wish we acknowledged that mental health is a struggle for many.

Caregiver Tips:

1. Know the signs and symptoms of mental health issues. Consult your pediatricians, school health staff, and counselors. (Note: Not all pediatricians are trained in mental health care. It's important to ask your pediatrician about their mental health experiences in combination with whole body health.)
2. Name risk factors in your family, treating them as you would physical health. For example, if diabetes runs in your family, you might be on the lookout for symptoms and inform your child of the history. *Our family has a history of diabetes. We need to be on the lookout for symptoms including but not limited to unquenched thirst, having to pee more than usual, or numbness in fingers or toes. And we have a history of depression therefore we need to be mindful of ongoing sadness, change in interest in activities, and more.*
3. Become a diagnosis vocabulary detective. Listen for the diagnostic words in use by others and by you, and thoughtfully replace with descriptive or appropriate words.

Educator Tips:

1. Know enough about signs and symptoms of mental health concerns to know when to refer a student for more support.

2. Listen for the diagnostic words in use by colleagues, students, and yourself.
3. Replace diagnostic words with observations of behavior. Often when writing comments about students we are advised to focus on behaviors and resist diagnostic words.

DEBATING EMOTIONS

I often ask students what is and what is not helpful to hear when upset. The top five comments on the unhelpful list were:

1. Calm down. (One student said she has never seen anyone calm down when told to do so.)
2. You have no right feel (fill in the blank), or I disagree with your feelings.
3. I can tell you feel (fill in the blank).
4. You should feel (fill in the blank).
5. I am sure (fill in blank) didn't mean it.

Whether verbally or visibly expressed (via body language, facial expression, and more), experiences elicit feelings. When someone is upset, the natural reaction is an attempt to comfort and assist, but sometimes our desire to help may cause the feelings to go underground. It would have been easy to tell Lex not to worry when she expressed her concerns about tuition, math grades, and saying goodbye to her friends. But that response may silence or force feelings into hiding. It would not have made the concerns disappear.

Stuffing feelings down is like holding beach balls underwater; eventually, they come to the surface with force, spilling

Making time to identify and respond to ar

others will ultimately expend less time an

Tips for avoiding the debate:

1. Avoid directive comments associate
2. Engage empathy, relating to the exp
3. Listen to hear (see Listening to Hea

[handwritten note: ⤷ re-affirm feelings, try to understand the scene, also]

[handwritten note: ⤷ mental health signs & symptoms]

55

4. Ask yourself, "Is my reaction to debate someone's feelings because their feelings bring up emotions in me?"

"You can never go wrong by validating a child."

Phyllis Fagell

11

Acknowledge Now, Address Later

When a comment needs to be acknowledged but you can't fully address it in the moment

↳ prepare follow up message to create security/ care for the class and/or student

Sometimes we don't know how to respond in the moment, and we choose to address it privately, later. More than any other, teachers state they prefer addressing in private. One of the numerous challenges to addressing an event in private is the students who saw or heard the comment are unaware that it has been acknowledged creating uncertainty at best within the larger class dynamic.

We can bridge the gap and acknowledge pivot topics in the moment and space where they come up while still addressing them at a different time and place. For example, telling a class a comment was heard and it will be addressed with the student privately. In that situation, a follow-up message is essential and can be powerful, especially if it's a message that is co-constructed with the student who made the original comment. Randolph Carter, a diversity practitioner and founder of East Ed, advises teachers, "We need to acknowledge something happened, even if we do not know how to respond. It is far better to stop, say you need to think about your response, than not respond at all."[1] And we don't have to wait until we

---

1 Randolph Carter, East Ed

have the perfect response. By asking for a few minutes to think, we both acknowledge the weight of the matter and give ourselves time to think. My colleague at Friends Academy, MaryJo Allegra, calls this 'the power of the pause.'

12

Use Code Words

Words to help kids ask for help in front of friends without anyone catching on

The text reads, "I am having a great time, can I stay longer?" Anyone who saw this text (either by looking over the boy's shoulder or seeing the parent's phone) would assume everything is good and he was asking to stay longer. But he wasn't. He was feeling socially awkward and needed a rescue without losing dignity. His text communicated the need. His mom understood; she knew because they had talked beforehand and established a code, 'Great.' Seeing great in a text meant her son was uncomfortable and needed to go home. Mom lovingly played the bad guy and responded that no he could not stay and she was on her way to pick him up giving her son what was needed.

Code words aren't just for caregivers. Teachers have successfully used code words to remind a student to adjust their behavioral choices without having to publicly call out the behavior in front of the whole class. Advisors have used code words so a student can communicate their needs without sharing them among the entire advisory. Similarly, coded actions can be helpful. For example, a teacher using the coded cue of walking by the student's desk and lightly knocking on it as a cue to attend to the discussion. In this case, the student was known for overexplaining and in so doing, frequently received a negative reaction from peers when raising his hand. When walking around the classroom, the teacher gently tapped his desk to indicate that he was overexplaining. This code was co-developed with the student and helped him moderate his behavior and reduce negative responses from peers.

Code words support both you and your child. And they respond to one of the biggest drivers of adolescent behavior: fitting in. Adolescents, by nature, rarely want to be the odd one out, seem weak or awkward in front of their peers. Code words are an easy way for kids to communicate concerns while saving face in front of their friends. If any of his friends read the text to his mom, the boy would still hold onto his dignity in his peer group. And if they read his mom's response, they would assume his mom was strict and would have no idea of their classmate's concerns. Using code words empowers the child to assess their comfort levels honestly and gives them a hidden ally and code words provide caregivers with a tool to support their child that can also help unpack how their child is navigating their social life.

Tips for code words:

1. Find a time to establish a code word separate from the situation that may call for it.
2. Co-create with the child:
   a. The code word
   b. The adult response
3. Ensure the word piques no interest. The term "great" draws no curiosity, whereas a phrase such as "bananas" is clearly out of place and will elicit questions.
4. Establish a time afterwards to discuss what prompted the use of the code word.

Don't assume our friends are our primary influence on who we will become. We are learning by watching adults too. Know we need support to help us discover who we are so we can have a strong belief system supported by caregivers even if it is different than what you want us to be.

Student's advice to adults

13

Remembering Pluto

As we learn, we Change how we respond

To paraphrase Maya Angelou, you make the best decision you can with the information you have, and when you know better, you do better. If you read a story or strategy in this book and regret how you handled a situation in the past, remember Pluto.

For most of my life, if I made a solar system without the planet Pluto, I was wrong. Then if I made a solar system *with* Pluto, I would have been wrong. Now, as scientists continue to make discoveries, we aren't so sure. We need to allow ourselves to have our own *Pluto* moments as we stretch and learn. While we take time to reflect and learn lessons, it is also important not to spend too much time feeling badly, dwelling on what we might have done differently. Limiting our time frees us to up learn the necessary skills so as not to repeat the behaviors.

Reflection question:

Consider moments when you felt certain about something and then adjusted that certainty with new information. How did it feel? What factors helped you to move past it?

If we can share our story with someone who responds with empathy and understanding, shame can't survive.

Brené Brown, *Daring Greatly*

14

Multiple Access Points

Getting to the root of the concern through a variety of avenues

In general, a bike trail begins at one point, ends at another, with multiple entry points along the way. This allows riders to join in and hop off at the most convenient spot. Conversations, like bike paths, also have numerous access points.

Corrective conversations gear toward changing behavior. Collaborative conversations focus on deepening understanding. My first effort for entering either collaborative or corrective conversations is at the most subtle point, increasing the message as needed. Imagine a number line of one to five, with one being the most subtle, and five being the most intense in a collaborative conversation or the most direct in a corrective one.

Noticing students running in the hall I might say in a slightly louder than usual voice, that I must have imagined students running in the halls because they know that they should not do so. In this manner, I am not calling on students directly, laying the expectation, and using a moderated voice is a one on the corrective scale. Often, students stopped running. When they didn't, I would increase the message, calling them by name and clearly stating the expectation. Saying something along the lines of 'for safety reasons, Alex and Amy, I need you to walk to class' is a three on the scale. On the rare occasion the running continued, my message deepened (as did my voice) and became more direct. A four on the scale would be, "Alex and Amy, stop running in the hallway, and if that is hard for you, you will walk to classes with a teacher." A five on the scale would be delivering consequences for their actions.

Collaborative conversations focus on learning and understanding. An example of increasing directive on the scale of one to five comes from a conversation I had with a student who was increasingly disengaging from class. Our faculty wanted him to engage and to understand why he seemed distant. Collaborating with the student meant telling him the topic of our concern and scheduling a mutually agreeable time for us to meet (see the Use One Sentence section).

> **We can always increase the strength of the message but we can rarely decrease the impact of going too big too soon.**

A teacher asked a student a one question on the collaborative scale 'we have noticed you seem less engaged in class. Can you tell me what you have noticed?' The student then shared the challenges he was having at home, that one of his parents recently lost their job, and how his other parent had to start working the night shift. The student wasn't sleeping well and he was worried about his family's financial security. By offering a chance to open up (rather than a directive to work harder), he was able to speak his truth and we were able to create a support plan that served his needs.

This subtle, level one approach invited the student to share his concerns. A stronger approach or directive ("wake up, get back to work") might have been a faster, in-the-moment reaction, but it would have overlooked the actual issues at play. By choosing a softer entry point to a conversation, we invite a student to be part of the problem-solving, instead of being its target.

We can always increase the strength of the message but we can rarely decrease the impact of going too big too soon.

15

Creating Menus

Developing a list of options for addressing situations

Creating menus between kids and caregivers and between kids and teachers stimulates collaboration and helps both parties feel heard. Menus are creative, communicate boundaries, and should reflect your values. To construct a menu, we:

1. State the need or problem using the one-sentence strategy to ensure clarity.
2. Determine a limited amount of work time to maximize idea generation and minimize disagreement.
3. Brainstorm ideas. Taking turns, all involved add thoughts to a list. All views are welcomed at this stage—so no crossing off, no saying something won't work, or disapproving facial expression.
4. Review of the list. Each person can only delete ideas they contributed; they can ask questions about the other views.
5. Ask which ideas are feasible and within your purview? For example, expelling a classmate is not something a student, caregiver, or teacher can do. But alerting the administration of ongoing challenges with that student is appropriate.
6. Choose a couple of options to implement as soon as possible.
7. Schedule a follow-up meeting to review the strategy's success or lack of success and determine the next steps.

Menu development can happen quickly and is dependent on feasible options. I think of menus as the inside of a corral with the fence being the boundaries. Growing up riding horses to school, we learned to build corrals outside our homes.

Corrals provide boundaries containing the horses but within the corral, the horses could roam freely. The corral represents the options you are comfortable with and space to range represent the choices for the students to claim. For example, we must have a family meeting today (boundary) and we will create the agenda together (choice). Menus provide multiple options, ensure a check-in point to choose another option if the first was not successful or to celebrate progress.

16

Check-in Before Checking Out

The importance of scheduling time to review progress

Have you ever left a conversation and then thought of all the brilliant things you wish you had said? This to be especially true of tense conversations. Creating check-ins offers us opportunities to add, revisit, and refine our messaging.

Toward the end of any conversation, schedule a check-in time to follow up. These check-in times work best when co-scheduled and the agenda is known. Topics might include sharing additional reflections or discussing the attempted problem-solving strategies. Reviewing what has and hasn't worked during a check-in meeting allows you to glean new information and share how both of you are feeling after some processing time has passed. You might even use the time to celebrate a positive outcome. Scheduling check-in time also avoids the potential emotional strain a young person might feel later when they are unexpectedly asked to revisit a conversation.

17

Deepening the Parent – Caregiver – Teacher Partnership

Linking the adults to support the kids

Educators have you even felt a change in direction was needed but worried the parents would object? Caregivers, have you ever wanted to call school but didn't want to be *that* parent?

Parents, caregivers, and teachers have the same goal. We want to help each child develop healthy relationships with themself, with learning, with their peers, and with the school community. Parents, caregivers, and teachers know children in different contexts—home and school. We also have different perspectives on how to meet our shared goals, and those perspectives can lead us to avoid challenging yet essential conversations (or worse, turn those conversations into conflict). Avoiding doesn't give our kids the support they need and deserve, in either celebrating their accomplishments or identifying potential struggles.

Ideas for creating a caring parent–teacher relationship that benefits our kids:

1. We embrace that we get to co-create, and we decide what kind of relationship we want to have. We ask, "Do we want to be a community of people who complain about each other? Or do we want to be a community who works

69

together toward our shared goals?"
2. From this shared understanding, we assume the best in each other, communicating directly rather than talking about each other with others.
3. We support each other, genuinely asking how can we best meet our shared goals? We co-construct the plan to meet as many of our goals as possible. When we are confused or challenged, we ask how to clear up the confusion or meet the challenge. Simply put, we resist assuming the other is not fulfilling the role of caregiver or teacher.

A key factor for kids flourishing is the absence of loyalty conflicts. A loyalty conflict refers to a child stuck between conflicting messages and values between home and school. Common language reduces the number of loyalty conflicts between home and school. Typically, we as caregivers have a cursory view into what is happening at school, and educators similarly have limited information about students' home lives. Asking questions, inviting curiosity and collaborative thinking, and providing advance information helps to reduce the chance of a loyalty conflict.

Avoiding loyalty conflicts does not mean caregivers and teachers need to be in complete agreement. In fact, kids need to see adults be able to disagree while maintaining a relationship. While we disentangle loyalty conflicts, we acquire skills to work through the hard stuff for the better of everyone involved. Some tips for avoiding loyalty conflicts include asking questions, looking for overlapping areas of agreement, and voicing or venting concerns outside the earshot of kids.

By elevating what is going well (no matter how small) we can better ground the caregiver–teacher relationship in communicating care for the student.

18

To Call or Not to Call

Tips for deciding whether and how
to call the school or home

Teachers and administrators commonly hear concerns from caregivers with the caveat that their child cannot know they called. Caregivers know the school will be helpful but worry how their child will react. And we educators want to help but are challenged when we cannot act on information we now know. We all miss a chance to provide partnered assistance. Similarly, educators may tell caregivers what is happening without telling the student.

One way kids meet their need to fit in is by stating opposition or displeasure. Allowing your child/student to go on record as not wanting you to call school may ultimately bring them closer to you. For example, learning Rose was being treated poorly by her teammates, Rose's mom told her she would call the coach. Her mom did not *ask* Rose if it was OK to call, however she did say that if doing so was harmful she would not call. When teammates later asked why Rose why mom called, Rose could save face by expressing disagreement with her mom secretly grateful the coach was involved.

We can draw similar boundaries for kids while also allowing choices. When creating menus for response, caregivers might add 'call the school' as an option. Once other options are exhausted the caregiver can say a call must happen but give the choice of which teacher to call. Stating a call is needed while giving choices for who to call, the caregiver provides options within boundaries. Similarly, a teacher, acknowledging the student doesn't want a call home, might ask the student which caregiver to call and work to develop together the talking points. These examples create boundaries, allow students to save face, and offer choices.

Caregiver tips for contacting school:

- Tell your child a call is needed without asking for approval.
- Offer choices such as who to call and when to do so.
- Share observations: "I have noticed..."
- Ask if the school has noticed anything of concern.
- Inquire about available resources.
- Plan for follow-up.
- Inform your child.

Educator tips for calling home:

- Tell the student you will contact home.
- Allow choices of who to call and when to do so.
- Call early enough in the day to update the student and provide the caregiver time to process.
- Provide observations, for example 'we have noticed he isn't talking in class, has his head down a lot, and isn't talking to friends.'
- Avoid conclusions such as 'your child seems depressed.'
- Offer resources such as 'our school counselor has been a great help to many of our students, and I think a referral is necessary. Would you like me to put you in touch?'
- Invite partnership such as 'it's so hard when our kids struggle. Would you like to talk tomorrow to see how we can work together to support your child?
- Update the student on the conversation.

19

Hearts With Legs

Recognizing our children as our vulnerability

'I want to fix it for her. It's not right for her to have to deal with it!' declared a parent in our school, reminding me of a favorite saying of our children's preschool director akin to 'we know your children are your hearts with legs' and acknowledged Meg's foundational emotional connection—her desire to protect her child even from a distance. Over the years of using the heart with legs metaphor adding 'walking around out there in the world.' Parenting patterns labeled *helicopter*, *snowplow*, and *bulldozer* describe hovering above children at all times, clearing a path, or removing all challenges or even potential challenges. Challenges refer to life's ups and downs, not harm or trauma. These examples of desires to protect seeking to remove all barriers perceived to be in their child's way. They ensure caregiver involvement in every aspect of their children's lives. In other words, seeking to be the skeletal and muscular system around our hearts with legs walking around out in the world.

Protecting our children and students from challenge may feel like the right thing at the moment, but it also messages ineptitude on the part of the child. Raising and educating kids with all barriers cleared from their path communicating lack of confidence in their ability to deal with challenge or the caregiver is needed for function. This approach robs kids of valuable learning experiences and even struggles, necessary to grow up healthy. Raising and educating kids to be independent, to be strong, and to find their unique place in the world requires experiencing appropriate levels of challenges, making mistakes, learning problem-solving, and approaching tricky situations confident in the ability to deal with them. That can best happen if they gain practice doing so in a safe, nurturing home school environment.

Part Three

Responsive HUB Mindsets and Strategies

Responsive strategies help us look back and lean forward, taking the lessons of our experience and applying them to our future interactions.

20

"Fine" Is Not a Feeling

Expanding the use of feeling vocabulary

Robert was fully prepared for his eighth-grade presentation, the final project marking the end of middle school. He had thoroughly researched his topic, created responses to even the most obscure questions, and practiced where he would stand with his props. Robert's teacher asked how he felt as she walked by, nodding when Robert answered that he was fine before turning his attention back to his notes.

Like Robert, we often use non-feeling words such as *good, fine,* and *OK* instead of feeling words such as *nervous, excited,* or *intrigued.* These non-feeling works invite listeners to interpret them through their worldview. Similarly, the use of non-feeling words usage increases the likelihood of feelings being overlooked. In this case, the teacher with a long list of tasks analyzed *fine* to mean prepared and comfortable, concluding all was well. But Robert was struggling. True, he had done his work and felt ready, but he was also anxious, causing his voice to shake and a river of sweat to run down his back. The ambiguity of the exchange, combined with the teacher's interpretation of meaning, eliminated her opportunity to assist Robert.

'Fine' as a response to being asked how we are is a less extreme example of non-feeling word usage. In this case, the question 'How are you?' is not an inquiry about the state of emotions. These common exchanges signal a greeting but not truly inquiring how the person asking the question is feeling at that time. Similarly,

77

the response *fine* acknowledges the other person but is not a declaration of one's state of being. These touchpoints are fundamental to our everyday interactions. But they shouldn't be mistaken for something more in-depth than saying 'hello' or as an actual read on a person's emotional well-being.

There are plenty of moments when it is inappropriate or even unsafe to share our full range of emotions and feelings with everyone. And there are other moments when we do not have enough time to process anything more complex than *fine*. The goal, though, is to accurately recognize our feelings and either replace non-feeling words with true expression or, perhaps, eliminate the false solicitation of emotions (How are you?) with a direct acknowledgment (Good to see you!).

Checking-In Activity:

Reserving 'How are you?' to moments of genuine inquiry, what words might you use to greet someone and use as a response to a greeting?

1. Recall or imagine a situation in which you offered a non-feeling word.
2. Visualize your emotional experience as a lake with a still and calm surface representing the word *fine*
3. Imagine someone asking you at that moment how you feel. What would your immediate response be?
4. Take another three-by-four breath (in through the nose for a count of four, hold for a count of four, out through the mouth for a count of four).
5. Look below the surface of the lake, imagining each foot of depth as a different feeling. What feelings might be in each layer?
6. If you could redo this moment:
   a. What might you keep?
   b. What might you change?
   c. Would another person know how you feel? If so, how?

7. As you go through your day, take note of the non-feeling words used by both you and the people around you.

21

Expanding Feeling Vocabulary

Using more and better descriptive words to communicate feelings

Over the past three decade of school counseling, I have noticed an increase in what I think of as the "ad" feelings—a trend in which we use fewer, less descriptive feeling words such as sad, mad, glad, or bad. The downward arrow technique helps us move through vague feelings and connect with the emotions that are guiding so much of our behaviors.

To visualize the downward arrow technique, imagine an upside-down triangle or pyramid. At the top, the widest part of the pyramid holds the words and feelings most commonly used and most socially acceptable. It's worth noting that socially acceptable expressions of emotions are profoundly influenced by gender, age, race, culture, and more. As we descend, the pyramid narrows, and the feelings become more private and vulnerable. The bottom-most point of the upside-down pyramid holds the most sensitive feeling and informs our responses. Unaddressed, this feeling risks morphing into a "reaction emotion."

A common reaction emotion is anger, developing only after experiencing (and often ignoring) something more vulnerable such as fear or embarrassment. The downward arrow technique helps us identify the feeling(s) at the pyramid's point, allowing us the opportunity to redirect it, as demonstrated in the following scenario with my youngest, Mel.

"I am so mad, what a jerk!" declared Mel. A classmate loudly said that the diversity committee's Pride month display was ugly. (June is recognized as Pride month, promoting equity for the LGBTQIA+ community) (see the section 'what is different for kids today'). Mel and diversity committee members had worked hard to create meaningful and educational displays each month. Understanding Mel's anger as a reaction to more sensitive feelings, I acknowledged the feeling of frustration at having hard work evaluated in such a biased and basic way, and later asked Mel if there were any other feelings before anger. After a bit, Mel shared feeling embarrassed, hurt, and nervous caused by an uncertainty around how the other student felt about LGBTQIA+ diversity. Once attended to, the intensity of the anger lessened to a manageable level.

Getting to the tip of the pyramid can be complex. It's important to note, if our questions feel like therapy or an inquisition, they will likely backfire. The situation might be best supported by acknowledging the anger and leaving it as a placeholder or an invitation for a future conversation during a less intense moment.

Caregiver example:

A friend's parenting technique is to remind her children that even if our anger takes up all our time and energy, the emotions at the bottom of the pyramid will eventually need attention. She acknowledges the anger and offers to help asking her children what happened before they were anger (asking for concrete examples of what might be seen if watching the situation on a film helps her children to get out of some of the emotion). Early in her parenting, it sometimes took hours or even days to dig past the anger and arrive at the more vulnerable feelings. But with time, practice, and trust, she noticed that less "angry time" was needed with each new incident.

Educator example:

A student was having difficulty participating in group projects. Noticing a pattern, the teacher asked how the student feels when working in a group (a top of pyramid question). The student said wanted a social life outside of school but felt she would never have one. The teacher empathized gently, asking if there anything else going on (downward arrow question). Throughout the conversation, the teacher learned the student didn't know how to make friends and pushed others away before they pushed her away. Through the downward arrow and one-sentence strategies (see Use One sentence), the teacher increased trust and gathered enough information to support the student meaningfully.

Our emotions are the first line of response to challenging situations. By working with our children to process their emotions, move past anger, and find the heart of their feelings, we are teaching them resilience, self-discovery, and self-empowerment. It isn't about "not feeling." It's about sorting and processing our feelings so we have conscious and deliberate reactions. Navigating feelings is a process, and takes time. But in the long run, the time and energy spent being angry returns on our children (and us). By honoring one another's range of emotional experiences, we're creating a healthier environment.

Feeling Vocabulary Activity:

1. Incorporate a broader feeling vocabulary into the language (see list below). One idea comes from a teacher who has students take turns picking and defining a new or underutilized feeling word. The students know if the teacher hears it used correctly in a sentence during the day, they get a piece of candy.
2. Use the downward arrow as a map to identify the most visible to the most vulnerable feelings.

'Supporting one another is of utmost importance. Friendship should not be about competing with one another or feeling like you have power over someone else. Friendship is not about having someone fear you or follow your orders. Friendship should be about mutual respect, shared interests, and loyalty. It is nice to have someone lift you when you're feeling down, but it is even more important to have someone who will celebrate you when you are at your best. That is a sign of a true friend.'

Lauren Keller

List all visible behaviors such as acting out

List all visible feeling(s) - do not use 'anger'

List fewer and more vulnerable,
less visible feeling(s)

One or two vulnerable
feelings driving the behavior

Quiet Sad Finicky **Down** Sneaky *Sick*

Healthy Energetic Nurturing **Humorous** Dedicated

Talented **Blissful** Curious Empty **Inspiring** Stressed

Dazed Angry *Pained* Insecure Indifferent Wronged

Sleepy GleefulDesperate Grieved Questioning Prepared

Faithful Lonely Average **Depressed** Worried

Rebellious Controlled Relieved **Immature** Happy

Careful Nosy Strong Optimistic Fulfilled

Meek *Stricken*

FEELINGS

Confident Indignant **Young** *Honest* Imposing

Foolish YoungUnderstanding *Unstable* Enthusiastic

Spunky Cranky Arrogant **Enraged** Successful Unassuming

Untruthful Uncontrolled Trustworthy Scared Joyous

Fussy Unbalanced Attractive Dreamy **Imaginative**

Vicious *Mature* Up Complete **Challenged**

Content Merry Unattractive Intelligent Needy Well Old

Important Anxious **Meaningful** Furious Failure Destined

Trusting Bashful **Insightful** Amazed *Humble*

22

Can We Take That Again?

Scripting or preplanning your responses

Wouldn't it be great to redo a conversation so we can get it right? An actor in a show or movie may do multiple takes until they speak the lines correctly. In theater, the actors will rehearse for weeks or months to prepare. While we can't quite "rehearse" for our lives, we can prepare ourselves through a process called scripting. Scripting allows us to develop an appropriate response when an incident or event leaves us at a loss for words. The keys for scripting are:

1. Create only a few scripts.
2. Address the topics you wish you could do over.
3. Ensure scripts reflect your values.
4. Be brief.
5. Practice your lines.

Knowing I have a prepared response during challenging discussions has made scripting one of my most empowering strategies. Scripts allow a moment to think while acknowledging the other person.

Sample scripts:

The (topic, task, other) is new to me. When I was your age, I didn't learn to talk about this, so I am learning from and with you (see sections managing mistakes and creating intentional norms).

The topic is so important. It deserves more time and attention than I can dedicate right now. Can we schedule a time now for me to get back to you? Note: Sticking to the scheduled time is important.

Write Your Script Activity:

1. Think about a conversation in which a script might be helpful.
   a. Why is it difficult?
   b. Are there groups of people with whom it is more challenging?
2. Check-in with your PLOF.
3. Clarify your intentions.
4. Determine and write what you would *like* to say to convey your intentions.
5. Condense your intentions into a sentence.
6. Practice and revise your script until your intentions and impact are as close together as possible.

Below is an example of my script process:

1. Think about a conversation in which a script might be helpful.
   An adult in a workshop continually challenging the information I am providing.

   a. Why is it difficult?
      It causes me to question myself, I am mindful that others are watching, and I want to engage this person in a forward-thinking manner.

   b. Are there groups of people with whom it is more challenging?
      Yes, I find it more challenging when it is a man.

2. Check-in with your PLOF.
   My PLOF is in my stomach. It feels like I have a kaleidoscope of butterflies in my belly.

3. Clarify your intentions.
   a. Demonstrate we can talk across differences.
   b. Don't let my nerves get the best of me.
   c. Listen intently for areas of agreement.
   d. Be clear.

4. Determine what you would *like* to say to convey your intentions.
   I hope we can talk across differences and learn from each other. It's difficult to do so when the challenges are one after the other without think time between. I want to find areas we can agree on or at least adjacent thoughts.

5. Write your script down.
   I am a ponderer hoping to learn from others. It would be helpful to hear your concerns on a sentence. I will then think about them and will get back to you after the break.

6. Practice and revise your script until your intentions and impact are as close together as possible.

Some of my favorite "go-to scripts":
- This (word, understanding, idea) is new to me. Therefore, I am learning.
- Can you tell me what that (word, idea, understanding) means to you?
- This requires time and thought. I am short on both right now and don't want to rush. Can we schedule another time? (Be sure to schedule and keep the time.)

23

Take the Smallest Step Possible

Growth becomes sustainable by building on small steps

My college graduating class at the Catholic University of America was quite large, but my program within the School of Social Work was tiny (about ten students). I reveled in the size of our program. It afforded time to fully explore the theories and therapeutic approaches valued by social workers and learn from our professors with a depth I didn't find in any of my other studies.

Among the most influential was our professor, Dorothy Van Soest. Dr. Van Soest was and continues to be an advocate in the most active sense of the word. Her classes focused equally on the root causes of societal problems and on addressing their outcomes. Homework assignments included attending protests and volunteering. Her expectation that students volunteer led me to a shelter for those experiencing homelessness, and to a lifelong commitment to supporting this vulnerable community. Dr. Van Soest felt strongly that social workers could not stand on the other side of the bridge, inviting their clients to come over. Social workers had to join their clients at their starting point, look at what was needed to take the next step, and then move in step with them. Once we take a step, we look back at our progress, look ahead to the next step, and repeat until we cross the bridge. Dr. Van Soest urged taking small, steady, and sustainable steps toward our goals.

Adults charged with being thought partners with our kids assist kids in breaking down significant matters to small, manageable steps. One of the hallmarks of early to mid-adolescence is their concrete reasoning (see the section on physical and emotional development), fluctuating between all and nothing thinking (i.e., situations are either good or bad, with little in between). At times this polarization challenges the ability to shift thinking and engage in problem-solving.

We can help kids see problem-solving as multiple, small, easy-to-negotiate steps. We first dispel the myth that there is always a solution that feels good. Some problems have solutions that meet all of our needs and make us feel better. But often the answer to a problem involves compromise and may mean choosing the option with the fewest adverse reactions.

Approach problem-solving with early adolescents by asking them to imagine the situation as a linear continuum. The present circumstance is point A, and the desired outcome is point K (or beyond). Points B through L represent the stepping stones in between problem and solution. I like to ask students to look at the goal and identify the next very small step they can take to move them toward that goal. We start by thinking about one or maybe two steps and determine what might be needed to take those steps. Lastly, we identify the signs we'll look for to know if and how the student has taken that step.

24

Is It a Pebble, Rock, or Boulder?

Empowering kids to self-assess the "size" of the problem

My former colleague Tim Croft developed a system titled "Pebble, Rock, Boulder" to help his young students think about their problems in terms of impact.

Pebbles are impactful but minor. We can carry them in our pockets and may even forget we have them with us. Pebble problems may require attention but not immediately and you may not need help with them.

Rocks are heavier, more challenging to move, and may weigh us down. Rock challenges need attention and may need assistance or support from a friend or adult.

Boulders are immovable. We can only go around or over a boulder. Boulder problems require immediate attention and direct support.

Tim's metaphor allows students to assess their situation for its weight and impact at the moment and is a helpful shorthand. A family I know uses "Pebble, Rock, Boulder," and they acknowledge that a pebble to one person might be a rock to another. They also know that the person with the boulder is the first to get support.

25

Backward Exploration

Looking back to identify the first concern

A parent told me he didn't want his child to feel guilty for being White. The statement while surprising but not shocking as it has echoed throughout the country. The parent was angry about the discussions, and I needed to unpack that anger to get to the heart of his concerns. Approaching the caregiver with the backward exploration strategy helps us arrive at the root concerns. Backward exploration is a series of questions beginning with the most passionate response and progressing backward to identify the source. These questions help us reflect on our reactions, exploring whether our values are engaged, or discomfort is the driving factor. For example, caregivers may react when they find out that their child's school engages in discussions with topics that the caregivers find complex or challenging. Examining our responses helps us better understand the origin of our concern and therefore better navigate the discussion.

"Understand prejudice comes from not understanding and know we want to understand. Don't shelter us from knowing things; it leads to prejudice and stereotypes because we'll learn everything from the media, friends, and rumors."

Students offering advice to adults

SENTENCE STEMS

Sentence stems are a common educational tool for both exploration and reflection. They can be used in the classroom or at home. Adults using sentence stems to support backward exploration offer the beginning of a thought and the child fills in the rest. Backward exploration uses the sentence stem, "Before that, what did you believe?"

The backward exploration strategy combined with the one-sentence approach (see Use One Sentence) allowed me to listen and learn from an upset caregiver and understand the source of his discomfort.

Me: Before you concluded teachers would shame your child for being White, what did you believe?

Caregiver: All this talk about race is racist because it highlights differences.

Me: Before the school announced summer reading about race, what did you think?

Caregiver: I didn't. We don't talk about race. My parents raised me to believe everyone is the same no matter their color.

Me: So, because you don't talk about race, you're worried that...

Caregiver: I'm worried my kid is going to feel guilty and ask me questions I don't know how to answer.

Like many adults this caregiver was raised with the absence of racial awareness, believing talking about race was racist. He also worried he would mess up if he so much as attempted to enter the discussion. Using one-sentence and backwards exploration strategies, we were able to identify the source of his concerns, then we could address the real concern.

In this example, the caregiver did not leave the conversation happy with the new direction, but that wasn't my goal. My goal was to find out *how* his beliefs stacked upon each other to create his forceful response, thus enabling us to create a plan to move forward. His anger was a response to strong feelings. Anger is a *reaction emotion* activated by feeling unheard; compelling many to become louder or solicit others to *our side*. My goal was to listen for the root and reduce the depth of his anger so that we could eventually have a collaborative learning conversation. The first step was listening for the causes of his anger and uncertainty. Once we knew the source of feeling, we were able to create a response plan with strategies for navigating feelings instead of falling back on anger. One of the most effective interventions to the fear growing into anger is to respond when fearful.

26

Mapping Our Way Through Feelings

Going through rather than around feelings

This section examines strategies for working through (instead of getting over) feelings. Before we discuss strategies, we need to name the foundation on which the process resides. First, feelings are simply a response to internal and external experiences. Second, feelings, (unlike behaviors), are never wrong. We cannot control our feelings, we can only control our actions in response to our feelings. Finally, to provide support and make our responses more manageable, we need to identify the multiplicity of our feelings. To navigate through our feelings and are better able to navigate through these feelings, we expand our understanding of feelings, thus expanding our repertoire of responses.

27

Welcoming the Conflicted Feelings

Exploring our multiple feelings in any given situation

Lex arrived at class with visible excitement gushing her joy. She had just opened her first college acceptance letter and was relieved to know she had somewhere to go next year. Of course, the natural response of faculty was an equally enthusiastic congratulations. Lex's teacher offered her good wishes and acknowledged the potential complexity of her feelings. She noted the omission of the range of feelings can bring about internal conflict and offered to be a resource. Noting potential emotional conflict provided an opening for Lex.

Lex thought for a few minutes and responded, "It would be a good school for me. But I'm also nervous about the lack of scholarship money; it's far from home, so it's not just tuition expenses to consider. I'm concerned about the acceptance being contingent on my end-of-term math grade, and even though we still have three months, I'm sad about leaving my friends."

The diversity of emotional responses to experiences such as Lex's excitement (happiness, nervousness, worry, concern, and sadness) is common. By underscoring the importance of the entire range, we can better connect Lex's behaviors, such as clinging to friends and staying up too late reviewing math problems, to their emotional origins.

Acknowledging the pivotal role of unexpressed feelings, helps students (and ourselves) to explore and navigate through powerful emotions. This process, in turn, reduces the capacity of those emotions to ignite negative or unconscious behaviors. By giving Lex the space to explore her complete emotional response, her teacher could both celebrate the positive news while simultaneously learning how to fully support Lex as she moved into this new phase of her life.

Multiple Feelings Activity:

1. Recall any challenging experience from the past week. It can be as quick as someone being curt in the grocery store or as lengthy as having a conversation about a weighty topic.
2. Check-in on if PLOF (see Gathering Parts and Tools section which describes your Physical Location of Feelings) was it activated. If so, did your PLOF inform your response? What was your reaction? What do you wish your answer could have been?
3. Take a three-by-four breath (through the nose for four, hold for four, release through the mouth for four).
4. Consider how you would (or did) respond if, at that moment, someone asked how you felt.
   a. If your answer is one feeling, what is it?
   b. Was it sufficient to focus on the one feeling?
   c. What are the unnamed feelings? And how might they inform your reaction?
5. Imagine you could have a "do-over," and the situation played out differently.
   a. Would your response have been different if this same challenge had occurred in a different environment? Or with another person? If so, how do you attend to the range of your feelings?
   b. Name all of the feelings you have.
   c. What would you change?

28

Location, Location, Location

Where we talk is almost as important as what we say

'It's about location, location, location,' said my mom. A real estate agent, mom was communicating that the financial value of a home is as much about where it exists as it is its architecture. Location is equally impactful when navigating conversations about challenging topics, especially when we consider shamed brains can't learn.

My son Logan offered "I always appreciated that the conversation always happened behind closed doors when I was in trouble. Getting in trouble was not a matter that occurred in front of other people, and it was even kept private from my sister, with the pact that I would not be part of her punishments, and she would not be a part of mine. When I did something wrong with my friends or around guests, my parents would take me aside for a minute and clearly tell me to stop whatever my wrongdoing was and save the rest of the conversation for home. In contrast, some of my friend's parents would openly scold their children before whoever was present, making an extremely awkward situation for everyone involved. I always liked that it was private because being in trouble was less about being embarrassed and more about learning from what I had done wrong. Also, it avoided the awkwardness of my parents having to enforce punishments in front of people we knew."

Caregiver Tip:

School counselor, Lauren Keller, advises caregivers that essential conversations occur in places where you are proximally close, with few distractions but not facing each other, such as a car or on a walk. Being near but not facing another allows you to hear each other and removes the vulnerability associated with eye contact. Being side by side also eliminates the pressure of monitoring your own and reacting to others' facial reactions.

Educator Tip:

As educators, we typically cannot take students in cars, so I offer walking meetings with them. Sometimes the walk is as brief as to the water fountain, and other times we may walk around the building. Because choice and privacy are paramount, I firstly offer students a few meeting place options and let them choose the most comfortable spot.

Head of School, Dana Harrison preceded me as the middle school principal. We have been friends for many years, and I have always welcomed his insights. I asked for advice on maintaining my principal role while forging relationships with students. Dana's face lit up as he suggested I get my CDL (commercial driver's license) so I could drive a bus. At our small school, faculty and staff filled as many roles as were needed, including bus driving. Dana loved being the bus driver, ensuring the kids arrived at field trips, and developing relationships with his students beyond principal and student. I didn't obtain a CDL, but I did talk to our bus drivers, who described deeply meaningful experiences with students as the first and last people associated with the school to see them each day. Some drivers who had driven the same route for years watched as their passengers grew-up, having a unique insight into their development.

Dana and the bus drivers, caregivers in a car, and educators walking shoulder to shoulder understand the choice of location for discussions can lead to more meaningfully connections with students.

29

Pivot Topics

Responding to off-topic comments

Location is equally important when addressing pivot topics. Pivot topics refer to the out of the blue topics with the potential to take the discussion in a starkly different direction. For example, as I taught a class on understanding equity in friendships, one of my students stated that equity was important but he was really just mad at his dad. As caregivers and educators, we likely have experienced a moment when a child brings up a topic, makes a statement, or asks a question that stops or redirects the focus. Many teachers and caregivers report their responses they freeze, don't say anything, tell a student not to say something again, or addressing the matter privately later. These same caregivers and teachers report these responses are inadequate.

Rosetta Lee, a diversity practitioner, when a guest on my podcast, shared that telling a child not to say hurtful things while neglecting to explain why means they will learn not to say those words in front of you. And the child misses the lesson regarding the impact of the words. The child also then knows their words or actions have power but remains ignorant of their consequences.

We can meaningfully respond to pivot topics both proactively and reactively. Proactively, we can develop intentional norms (see Norms Happen section), specifically focusing on addressing challenging questions. And we can respond reactively by having a script ready to use for one of those moments (see Can We Take That Again?) such as 'That comment has a substantial impact. We need to address it.' If you have time to address it, please do so at that time. If you don't have time, you might use a script acknowledging that something was said and informing the group it will be processed such as 'that was an important statement, and we will talk about it privately before coming back to the group'. More than anything else, students say, not responding to a provocative topic is far worse than responding, messing up, and then processing. The interpretation of silence is unique to each person, but the interpretations are often described as negative or agreement with the statement, and rarely presume positive intent. Not responding sends the message that we're agreeing with what was said.

Three steps for responding to pivot topics:

1. Proactive:
    a. Create intentional norms for all gatherings including teams, classes, and more.
    b. Clarify your values.
    c. Talk about mistake making

2. Reactive:
    a. Acknowledge what was said.
    b. If able to do so, process in the moment, remembering shamed brains can't learn and focusing on co-constructing the environment for how people should be treated.
    c. If unable to process in the moment (see Acknowledge Now, Address It Later section):
        i.   Communicate assurance of follow-up.
        ii. Designate time to meet.
        iii. Gather support or resources needed for the discussion.

3. Responsive:
    a. Follow-up with agreements made
    b. Follow-up with lessons learned
    c. Take time to process feelings

30

Questions Require Answers

Focus on how, rather than whether or not, to answer

Children ask questions because they are curious. Children ask questions of adults because they trust we will answer. And children cease asking questions of the adults who respond with deflections or who don't respond at all. The question is not *if* we should react, but *how* to respond. The challenge is our adultism in this case, viewing matters through our experiences as adults, causing us to see the question through our lens. We often filter and respond to questions from our age and stage, jumping to the answer we think the child wants. But in our haste, we may misunderstand what the child seeks.

When I was an elementary school counselor, a teacher arrived at my office appearing upset, on a Friday afternoon. (Those who work at schools know these incidents always seem to happen on a Friday afternoon.) The teacher informed me that the first grade wants to know how babies are born and were not letting it go. I immediately felt stuck because I knew we could neither answer nor ignore their questions. On my way down to the classroom, I quickly went through my checklist of questions:

- Do we have a letter on file we can hand out at carpool?
- What have the kids learned in health to date?
- What do they believe to be the answer?

My answers of *yes, not much,* and *not sure,* did not calm my PLOF. As we gathered in a circle, I remembered the one-sentence and backward exploration strategies (see Use One Sentence and Backward Exploration), with one sentence at a time, the teachers and I learned that one of the children heard people eat babies to get them in their bellies, and another student shared babies came from airplanes. Through backward exploration, sentence stem 'before that, what were you talking about?' we learned the child adopted from China often heard about how her family flew to pick her up, so she believed babies came on airplanes. And the other child reading a Greek mythology with pictures and conflated pregnancy with eating babies.

We listened to our students, clarified the origin of their questions, and shared that babies come from many places to be with their families. We wrote a note for parents and caregivers suggesting they talk with and listen to their child's questions, encouraging them to use one-sentence answers and access the discussion from the most suitable and age-appropriate point.

We almost missed it! Our adult view of the question 'Where do babies come from?' was that the children were asking about conception not about concepts. These were transportation questions as described by author and sexuality educator Deborah Roffman. Imagine how confused the children would have been if the adults in their lives answered with details about reproduction when they just wanted to know if babies arrived by plane. Using these strategies, one parent told me about a time when her son asked how he got to be in his house. She told him, he came home in a car with his mom's and brother. This parent was not putting off her child. She was ready to answer additional questions and began with the answer most easily accessible for her child.

Another example of responding to the age and stage of the child comes from Jamal and Amy. When I arrived at the school the principal told me I would not work with the youngest students because *they may not be ready.* After observing my other classes, the principal invited me to work with the youngest students. Together Jamal, Amy, and I developed the following for the adults on the differences between equity and equality.

Amy and Jamal shared that they were four and a half years old and were going to talk about the differences between equity and equality and described our recess adventure. As members of a community, they keep shoes outside of the classroom and today the three of us mixed them up such that we each had one of our shoes and the shoe of another. Jamal could tie his shoes and had lace-ups. Amy learning to tie shoes had slip-ons, and I had heels. It was hard to get out to recess both because of our shoes and the need to learn to tie shoes. Eventually we made it to recess but only had a few minutes before needing to head back in to ensure being to class on time. Amy shared equality was important because everyone should have shoes and was followed by Jamal who said everyone also needed shoes that fit and could be put on quickly.

"Children begin to notice difference before their language fully develops. As adults we can support them best by listening to their questions and wonderings and stepping into the raggedy places of uncomfortable conversations. It's never too early to help young children recognize and respect the diverse people in their communities and to affirm that diversity."

Brenda Crawley

Tips for answering these difficult sorts of questions are:
1. Attend to your PLOF.
2. Use one sentence (see section on Use One Sentence).
3. Assume the question asked is through the child's age and stage.
4. Ask backward exploration questions to ascertain the origin(s) of the question to inform your response (see section on Backward Exploration).
5. Listen to hear (see seen sections on Listen to Learn and Listening to Hear Instead of to Respond).

31

Body Language

Our nonverbal communication says more than we may think

While research varies, the London Image Institute posits that 93% of our communication is nonverbal, referring to it as "the 7% Rule, where all communication is only seven percent verbal and an overwhelming 93 percent non-verbal, specifically, body language and varying tones of speech."[1] Imagine a colleague turns to you with a smile, looks you in the eye and in an uplifted voice, asks, "Do you want to get a coffee after this meeting?" Now imagine the same colleague turned away from you such that you cannot see a full facial expression, her voice is flat, she is on her phone, and she asks (in a flat tone), "Do you want to get coffee after this meeting?" ending with a slight sigh. In both, the words are the same. However, the voice, facial expression, body language, make the two questions completely different. The messages are not in sync between non-verbal and verbal communication.

Misunderstanding or misinterpretation frequently derives from mismatched messages. The words used to invite you to coffee are lovely yet wholly undermined by the mismatch between spoken and unspoken language. Compounding the disconnect between verbal and nonverbal communication is how often we listen to *respond* rather

---

[1] How Much of Communication is Nonverbal? London Image Institute. 20 Mar 2020.

than listen to *hear*. Our body, resting face, tone of voice, cadence, preferences for processing, and speech habits expand this disconnect. Synchronizing our words with our reactions reduces the disconnect and can even create an empathetic response.

My colleague and friend Brooke Carroll and I frequently co-present workshops on navigating challenging topics. These difficult discussions are hard work and can easily be undermined by nonverbal communication. So, Brooke and I spend a good amount of our workshop unpacking the nonverbal factors that contribute to connection or disconnection. We focus on resting face, body language, habits of speech, and preferences for processing.

Body Language:
Thinking strategically about body language begins with identifying the intention. For example, if we seek to convey seriousness, we might face the person and sit at eye level with each other. A note on eye contact: Contrary to the commonly held belief that requiring someone to look you in the eye shows respect, forcing someone to look you in the eye forces compliance. Our conversation's intensity, comfort levels, and culture all influence the expectation to look someone in the eyes.

Resting Face:
Our resting face is the expression or body posture we have when not interacting or when we're thinking. My students and I were new to virtual learning and our theme was nonverbal communication. We looked for each other's resting faces and offered possible interpretations for each. My intention with students is to really listen. I am a pen and paper notetaker and when listening I put my pen down, often resting my chin on my palm. A student observed the impact of my pose can communicate disinterest. Disinterest is the furthest from my intentions and, thanks to my student, I now realize it and am working to break the habit.

Speech Habits:
Our cadence and inflections send multiple signals. "I think we should go to the store" sounds completely different if we raise our voice on the word "store," making it sound like a question versus if our voice is flat, which sounds like an observation. Similarly, a lowered voice at the end of a sentence, may sound like a command.

Preferences for Processing:

Are you at your best when you have some think time or when you can process aloud? Or are you more effective when answering in the moment? By understanding and naming our processing needs and preferences, we can better respond in situations that do not allow for those needs.

For example, I need think time but I've almost always held jobs that require quick on the spot decision-making. Adding the sentence stem, "I'd like think time, but see this is time-sensitive, so I am thinking and speaking" helps the listener and me to know the thoughts are not fully formulated. A colleague who processes verbally found adding the phrase "I am just thinking aloud here" reduced the misunderstanding that she was actively making decisions.

Unintentional Directives:

Listen for the unintentional use of directive words, such as verb choices inaccurately reflecting your intentions. When I was a principal our faculty and staff often attended conferences together. On the way back from one, a colleague asked how long my "to-do list" for her would be when we returned to school. We sat together during several sessions and inspired by the presenters, I took loads of notes and frequently exclaimed, "We should do that!"

Using the word *should* particularly when combined with the power imbalance of principal to teacher, she understandably thought I was telling her what we would do when we returned. Once she pointed it out, I began taking note of my frequent words with colleagues, staff, and children, replacing "should" with "that's something to think about." Sadly, I have no idea how many people experienced my enthusiasm as directives prior to her pointing it out. One tip is to invite a colleague to observe you can help to minimize these misunderstandings.

Camera Off:

Though not technically body language, COVID-19 and the Zoom classroom raised new questions about cameras being on or off. Many of these questions are similar to mismatched verbal and nonverbal communication. Liza Talusan, Ph.D., a strategic consultant and educator, writes, "For many, a home is a private place, separate from work, school, and life outside of its doors. Yet, virtual learning thrust teachers, leaders, coworkers, and peers into this private space. With a focus on content, curriculum, meetings, delivery, and engagement, the boundary between home and 'outside of home' quickly became blurred with little to no regard for how this boundary-crossing impacts the environment."

When a person feels exposed, it raises their anxiety. Increased levels of stress make tasks such as learning, teaching, parenting, and decision-making much more difficult. We might ask students how they can demonstrate their engagement with or without a camera. As we consider the lessons learned in remote learning, Talusan asks, "How did schools and organizations pay attention to the boundary-crossing that occurred during this time? What might schools and organizations do to engage in more culturally aware and responsive ways of entering into the home?" As always, administrators can ask teachers to share what has worked and what hasn't in their student, caregiver, and coworker interactions. Teachers can ask students what is and isn't working for them in the classrooms.

Body Language Tips:
These tips are for all of the above, and are not just about Zoom and cameras.

1. Ask someone to observe your resting face and body language for matching and mismatching messages.
2. Film yourself in a meeting. Ask a trusted person to watch the recording without sound, inviting them to tell you what your body language and facial expressions may communicate. Next, listen to the video without looking, paying attention to verbal cadence and habits of speech.
3. State what you seek to communicate. For example, I now tell people I am working to not rest my chin on my hand because it may express disinterest; it's a work in progress.
4. Create intentional norms (see Creating Intentional Norms), including:
   a. If in a virtual classroom or meeting:
      i. Clarify the required versus optional times for cameras to be on or off.
      ii. Allow students to express needs in the chat. For example, "My camera is off because a lot is going on behind me."

    b. Establish the expectations for device usage. I often ask attendees to name if they prefer notetaking on devices for in-person workshops, so their typing is not misinterpreted.

    c. With students, co-construct ways of communicating engagement whether in person or in a virtual classroom.

5. Monitor directive words.
6. Put words to your processing preferences and establish scripts such as "I need a few minutes to think" or "I am thinking aloud but not making a decision."

32

Talking in the Third Person

Talking to kids about others may be the best way to understand them

I once offered a class for caregivers called "How to talk so your child will listen" and another for their kids called "How to listen so your caregiver talks less." The skills were essentially the same for each group with the exceptions "*Give thirteen*" and "*Collect three.*"

Give Thirteen (for caregiver):

When we first see our child, we might extend a greeting and allow at least thirteen minutes before asking about their day. School days are long and exhausting; entire relationships can begin before the first bell and end by the last bell. Allowing time after school to settle provides a disconnect between school and home. I know of a mom who picks her daughter up from school each day. At the start of one year, she told her, "I know your day is long, and I am curious about every bit of it, but I also want you to have downtime. So, when I pick you up, I will greet and give you a snack and will then be quiet unless you want to bring something up."

Collect Three (for kids):

We strengthen relationships and deposit into our 'relationship bank' by sharing.

Understanding caregiver questions are not to be intrusive; they reflect a desire to know about their child's day often in the form of questions. One strategy is collecting three things during the day to tell caregivers thus reducing the number questions.

"How was your day?" a parent asks their child, who responds "fine." Getting a robust response from kids, especially if the topic is loaded, can be hard. Below is a list of questions we might choose from to broaden a child's answer (notice the questions start off lighter and increase in depth as you advance through them):

- Tell me one thing you noticed for the first time today. Or something you learned.
- What was the funniest thing you saw or heard today?
- If I were at school today, what might I see or hear?
- How are your friends?
- How do you imagine others your age are feeling?

And my two favorite questions:

- What do you think adults are misunderstanding? (Or how are adults unaware?)
- If someone your age (or in your situation) needed advice, what do you think might be helpful?

33

Be Willing to Be Blamed to Limit Your Child's Shame

Helping your child save face with friends may help them be closer to you

You being willing to be seen as strict may give your child more flexibility. A group of middle schoolers from Alexander Dawson Mountain School were guests on my podcast. Our topic was technology use, specifically what adults should know. The students reflected that they wanted more limits, even though they often acted like they didn't. One student summed this sentiment up by saying he may want limits, they are helpful... but he probably would not thank his parent for imposing them. The limits offered from all of the students ranged from wanting boundaries placed on screen time to wishing their caregivers would take away their device after a certain time of night.

To be sure, the digital-social landscape is nothing like the world most of us grew up in, and our children are often in situations that make them uncertain or uncomfortable. And often, those are situations that we, the adults, aren't prepared for because it falls outside our range of experiences. We can't always protect our kids, but we can offer ourselves as a means of protection by being the 'bad guy'. As a standing invitation, we regularly told our kids that they could and should use the script 'I know my parents won't let me do that"' any time they were in an uncomfortable situation. By shifting 'blame' onto us, they were protecting themselves both from the situation and from social embarrassment or stigma.

34

Listening to Learn

Differentiate between listening to respond and listening to learn

John, a parent at a parent–teacher conference declared that Allison just wasn't getting him. Allison, believing she did understand repeated back almost word for word what John had said. Recognizing the increasing frustration on both sides, Barb, the teacher, suggested, that she didn't believe they we were getting anywhere and asked to regroup and meet again later. Allison repeated John's words to demonstrate that she had listened to him. But listening to *respond* is not the same as listening to *understand*.

Often, and especially in difficult conversations, we find ourselves waiting for our turn to speak. Maybe we are really excited about the point we want to make or story we want to share. Or maybe we're trying to convince the other person that they're wrong. We'll jump at certain words or phrases, or spend our energy crafting our next sentence or argument instead of attending to the perspectives, stories, or arguments of the person speaking. In these moments, we're listening to respond. It's normal but doesn't engender meaningful communication.

On the other hand, listening to understand aims at creating an environment in which people are more likely to cooperate. It increases our ability to share and receive each other's viewpoints. By focusing on hearing a person and not just preparing our reaction or response—we can share our perspectives without engaging in conflict.

Guy Itzchakov and Avraham N. (Avi) Kluger have spent years studying interpersonal communication and its impacts on personal and professional growth. Their 2018 article in the *Harvard Business Review*, "The Power of Listening in Helping People Change," summarized some studies about the impact of listening in the workplace.

"We found that speakers paired with good listeners (versus those paired with distracted listeners) felt less anxious, more self-aware, and reported higher clarity about their attitudes on the topics. Speakers paired with undistracted listeners also reported wanting to *share* their attitude with other people more compared with speakers paired with distracted listeners."

Itzchakov and Kluger's workplace observations that "listening seems to make others more relaxed, self-aware of strengths and weaknesses, and more willing to reflect in a non-defensive manner" are also accurate for colleagues, caregivers, teachers, and students in home and educational settings.

In the article, "The Biggest Communication Problem Is That We Listen To Respond Not To Understand," Anthony Pica writes, "The gap between what is said and what we hear is also linked to how slow or fast a person speaks. The average person speaks 175 to 200 words per minute, but most people can listen to and process 600 to 1,000 words per minute. Because of this, our brain is not always entirely focused on what someone is saying and goes off in different directions, preventing us from understanding what is being said."

35

Listening to Hear

A four-step process toward understanding

Listening and hearing are two separate yet connected components toward understanding. Hearing a four-step process: 1) listen; 2) hear; 3) acknowledge; and 4) respond. Many of us jump directly from Step 1 to Step 4, missing the crucial middle steps. The middle two steps (hearing and acknowledge) create the capacity to hold weightier topics allow for the understanding or connection sought.

Step 1: Listen
Listening is data gathering. Listening is similar to building a transcript to capture what was said, in a manner that the speaker feels you correctly received the facts. When observing someone listening, we might see them facing or turning their head to the speaker. We may see note-taking or signs of processing such as looking up or nodding. **Listening is in the head. Listening is collecting facts or the parts of the message.**

Step 2: Hear
Hearing is processing. Hearing is putting the speaker's words into your vernacular. We might condense or add nuance, and the speaker still recognizes the essence of what they shared. When we observe someone hearing, we might see the speaker

communicating being understood by nodding their head. The person hearing might ask for clarification or further explanation.

One of my favorite questions is, "What do you feel I am not hearing or understanding?" This may feel challenging to ask and we may feel we have to brace for the answers. However, I have found, often the voice softens, the tension lessons, and we are better able to understand each other. **Hearing is in the ears and chest.**

> **Hearing a four-step process: 1) listen; 2) hear; 3) acknowledge; and 4) respond. Many of us jump directly from Step 1 to Step 4, missing the crucial middle steps.**

Step 3: Acknowledge

Acknowledgement is an affirmation connected to one or more emotions. Acknowledgement communicates, "I hear you, and I see the impact on you." Acknowledgment does not mean we must agree or cannot disagree; it is an empathetic response to something shared. When acknowledging others, we might reflect on the feelings we see ("That sounds painful") or ask the speaker how they feel. **Acknowledgement is in the heart and gut.**

Step 4: Respond

Responding may include action ("I need to talk to the teacher") or inaction ("This is a lot to take in, let's take a minute—for a break, drink of water, silence, other, etc.").

Listening to hear takes practice, but even our youngest children can move through all four steps efficiently with practice. The need to *fix* the situation for someone, especially when a child is involved, is a powerful driver. So powerful, it often moves us from listening right to responding without taking the time to hear or acknowledge. Students consistently share that given the choices of an adult fixing something for them or an adult hearing them, they would choose to be heard.

In the beginning, it might seem stilted or inefficient to move through all four parts of listening. But we've all witnessed or experienced moments when, in not being heard, someone experiences hurt or frustration that compound the emotions of the initial incident. PLOF can play a significant role here, sending stress messages that propel us directly into response mode (see the Physical Location of Feelings). **Responses are in the feet, hands, and mouth.**

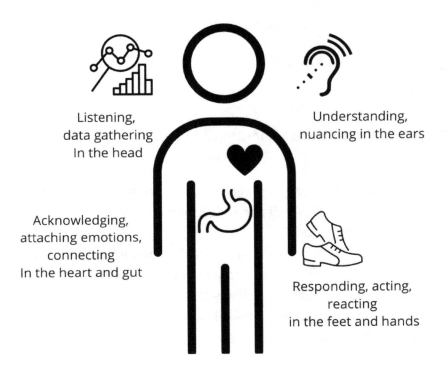

Listening,
data gathering
In the head

Understanding,
nuancing in the ears

Acknowledging,
attaching emotions,
connecting
In the heart and gut

Responding, acting,
reacting
in the feet and hands

"Listening helps others find their voice and gives more weight to your own."

Montanna Wilson

Understanding Activity:

1. Quickly read the following to yourself. Alfred, a fifteen-year-old says "This weekend, a ton of us went to the game and then to Jeff's house. Bob and Devon have liked each other since third grade and finally hooked

up. Everyone posted the coolest pics on their stories of staying up until sunrise. I can't wait to go to the game with them next week!"
2. What is your PLOF indicating?
3. Ask yourself how you would respond?
4. Reread the story, asking yourself:
   a. What was said?
   b. What was heard
   c. What was felt?
   d. How do you respond?

5. Does your answer change from Step 2 to Step 4?

When I first heard that story, my reaction was negative and full of questions. Why did you stay up all night? Were *any* adults present? What *else* was going on at this clearly out of control party?

But when we step back, what is Alfred really sharing? He's talking about an exciting night in which he felt socially connected. If, in my response, I jump to my judgements and concerns, Alfred will likely shut down or grow defensive.

So, after listening, I try to hear him—his enthusiasm and excitement for what happened and what might happen next in his growing social life. I acknowledge how important the night was for him.

Only after honoring what Alfred has shared with me do I build my response. Maybe I ask questions or get some clarifying details. After all, Alfred's only stated action in the story was to stay up all night (and possibly post pictures). We might not approve of everything that happened at Jeff's house, but if we open with that disapproval, we'll never hear another story about Jeff's house (or any other house) again.

Tip:

1. When someone is sharing with you, ask yourself:
2. What words are being used?
3. What does the speaker want me to hear?

4. Is my PLOF on alert? And if so, how will I respond?
5. What feelings arise?
6. Consider the previous questions asking, "How do I want to respond?"
7. Equally important is *who* is listening to us. The adolescent years mark significant physical, emotional, and chemical changes (see the section on developmental changes).

In the images below we see how quickly kiddos grow and change in middle years. The picture on the left was two weeks before middle school (sixth grade), and the picture on the right was taken a month after starting high school (ninth grade) at Laps for Lexi charity event, a group fighting childhood cancer. The person on the right has grown physically; the face and voice have changed, and he has developed more mature behaviors. However, in recognizing the unevenness of adolescence, we might consider when talking to the person on the right, it may be the person on the left who is listening.

36

End With the Beginning in Mind

Thinking about where you hope the conversation will go helps center us in the moment

The core of every relationship is built on trust. Trust allows us to share and confide, hear and feel heard, support and be supported. When we trust someone, we allow them in and they allow us in, and that process shapes us. For young people, the trusting relationships they build with their peers and their adults have an immeasurable impact on the people they become.

We build our caregiver–child and teacher–student relationships with every interaction we have. Like links in the bicycle chain connecting the gears, each touchpoint connects, moving the relationship forward. This section examines components of our conversations with young people, exploring strategies to support strengthening adult–child relationships.

Khyati Joshi, author, professor, and speaker offers these suggestions for forging relationships with students. First, get to know your students. Good teaching is learning who is in the room. Second, be inquisitive. Trust that we don't need to have answers to ask good questions.

You are in charge of your personal growth. What do you continue to study?

Johnnie Foreman

37

Culture Carriers and Culture Creators

Stop trying to convince each other and start looking for common ground

Kids test limits. It's part of their job of growing up. Even when we adults are correct, we will likely encounter tension when telling kids how to be and how not to be, or when our opinions dictate their actions. Even when they agree with us, kids will often double down on their position when they do not feel their viewpoint matters, ensuring kids and adults are on opposite sides of the bridge unwilling to move.

What if we thought of our polarized positions as two parts of a whole, each side essential for progress? I call these groups the *culture carriers* and the *culture creators*. The culture carriers often say things like, "We have done that before, we have always done it this way, and it works." The culture creators often ask, "Why not...?" "Can we...?" and "What about....?"

Culture carriers and creators are often in conflict, believing they need to win over or convince the other group. In reality, we need both creators and carriers. Groups don't do well if they repeat the same thing repeatedly, unwilling to grow in their learning. Groups also don't do well if they constantly innovate and do not give new ideas a chance to settle. When culture carriers and creators listen to each other and learn from one another, they find the areas where their goals overlap. These areas of overlap (think of the middle of a Venn diagram) can be expanded upon, effecting change in a supported and sustainable way. Culture carriers proceed across the bridge as they always have. Culture creators may want another route or not to cross at all. By collaborating, culture carriers and creators can learn from each other and develop the most robust system for going from one side of the metaphorical bridge to the other.

Common Ground Activity:

1. Look back on a moment when you found yourself on a side opposite of an issue as someone else.
2. Were you a culture creator or carrier?
3. Was the other person a culture creator? A culture carrier? Both?
4. Use the following diagram:
    a. List on one side the points of your position.
    b. List on the other side the attributes of the other person's position.
5. Look at both sides to identify areas of agreement and list these areas in the middle.
6. Ask how the areas of agreement can be expanded.

38

Preview

Looking to the future helps right the present

Jan's mom asked about class and received a forceful declaration that 'nothing happened, followed by a snappy question of why she was asking. Jan's mom's question was not an intended attack, but it was a surprise, immediately provoking Jan to defend herself.

When someone drops a challenging conversation in front of us, many of us recoil. We're unprepared and caught off guard. Having some preparation better allows us to approach the conversation with our thoughts first and foremost (rather than our feelings) leading to healthier communication.

Jan's mom reframed the conversation, stating she talked with Jan's teacher, understood things have been difficult, and that they should make time to talk. This approach introduced the topic and its importance while allowing Jan think time to get her thoughts organized. They will still talk, but now it can be a planned discussion and not as likely to be argument.

Even when we cannot schedule a future meeting, we can create a little space. Alexa, a math teacher, heard a student made an insensitive comment. Instead of jumping to her immediate, knee-jerk reaction of "That's not kind and cannot be said in this classroom," she said, "That was a hurtful comment, and we need to address it after class." This message alerted the student of Alexa's dissatisfaction giving him the heads up that they would be speaking shortly. It also signaled to the other student that the matter would be addressed.

By acknowledging the comment and impact in the classroom when it occurred, Alexa informed the rest of the class that she saw it and would respond. Believing shamed brains cannot learn, Alexa opted not to process the comment at the moment. After dismissing the class, Alexa thought the student needed an additional moment to think, so she told the student she would go to the bathroom and they would have the discussion when she returned.

Educator Tip:
Going to the bathroom or getting water is among my go-to's for taking a minute to think. Saying you need a bathroom break creates physical distance and provides a moment to reflect. Plus, it's difficult for others to challenge the need to use the bathroom.

CHOICES BUILD OWNERSHIP

Empowering children through giving choices has meaningful impact. In her book *Just Ask Us: Kids Speak Out on Student Engagement*, Heather Wolpert-Gawron writes:

According to the student engagement survey, student choice is listed as one of the most engaging strategies a teacher can allow in the classroom. Want to know how to engage students, enthuse them, and bring out their best effort? Want ways to differentiate organically? Give them a voice in their decisions. In a society that barely listens to each other, listen to our students. A system that can be a flood of top-down lets your classroom allow voices to trickle up. In our very classrooms, we have the brains that will solve tomorrow's problems, but to give them training means we have to give their neurons a chance to solve the issues of today. ... Student choice builds ownership in the learning, allows students to display their education in the way they feel best represents their knowledge and enforces true differentiation.

A menu of options empowers young people with strategies to help them navigate their world. They still have guidance and input, but they are addressing it for themselves.

Co-scheduling (or offering a choice for having "the hard conversation") empowers a young person. But we always have to remember to provide doable alternatives. If Tuesday is the only day you can connect, asking what day of the week they want to talk creates a false sense of options. You will either have to walk back to the Tuesday meeting time or try to meet at a time you don't have available. Offer options that offer choice within your boundaries. 'I have time on Tuesday. Would you like to talk before dinner or after?'

As described in the beginning, my oldest kiddo Logan offers insights. At age 11, Logan wrote the following about the importance of choice within limits when teaching decision-making skills:

> As I have grown up, there are many things that my parents have done that have gone unnoticed to me. Looking back on some of these things, I see how my parents taught me essential lessons and abilities. I don't know if my parents, at one point, decided to teach me to make decisions or if they began teaching me subconsciously. Whichever it was, the idea became very conscious and, at some times, seemingly constant. Parents teaching their children to make decisions creates a pathway for making important decisions later in life. I think that when big decisions are in their children's future, parents should tell them long in advance, giving them plenty of time to settle with an idea, so there is no surprise or refusal at the time of the decision. At first, my parents guided me through decisions, asking questions that guided me step-by-step through the decision at hand. For example, asking me where I wanted to go to dinner started a conversation that went something like this:
>
> "Where would you like to go to dinner?"
>
> "I don't know."
>
> "What kind of food do you want?"
>
> "A hamburger."

"OK, McDonald's or Burger King?"

"McDonald's."

By breaking these decisions down into more minor choices, I made the decision even when I didn't focus on making the entire decision on my own. Soon, I was able to take some of the steps out of the findings by communicating what I wanted. As more and more of the process became subconscious, I could easily break down more significant decisions on my own.

The most important test that I have come to so far came with my decision to go to boarding school. I had to break the decision down into weighing my education against friends, education against family, education against swimming, etc. It was hard. I had to fight to convince my parents that boarding school was a good idea, and while I worked to convince my parents, the idea became more and more concrete because as my parents became convinced, it left the decision solely up to me.

There are a few things that I wish my parents and I had done as I learned how to make decisions. First, I wish I had seen that my parents were teaching me to decide things. I only saw that my friend's parents didn't let them have as much freedom of choice as mine did. Second, it would have been helpful to me if my parents had broken down the decisions less and less as I learned to do that myself because it started to get annoying when my parents drew out the conclusions into so many small parts. If my parents had communicated that they were teaching me to make decisions, I think we could have avoided some problems. That way, I was conscious of the steps, and then I would have communicated to them that I already understood that step.

One thing that I truly appreciated at the time was that my parents respected my opinion on decisions regardless of my age. When I was younger, my parents considered moving because my mom received a very generous job offer. When they asked me about my opinion, I told them that I would not move. Where most parents would have made the decision themselves, my parents considered my opinion, and even though the decision was ultimately theirs, my opinion weighed heavily on the decision, with them eventually deciding that we would not move.

Another time, a few years after we decided not to move, my mom received another job offer. We, as a family, visited the school she was being recruited to and explored the idea of living there. This time when my mom asked for my opinion, I did not simply refuse. I thought through how it was a good and bad idea and then presented my thoughts on the decision. With this decision, I had become part of such an important decision.

Giving kids choices creates space for them to practice skills, and time for us to observe their progress.

"What I most hope you know about being in middle school is that at all times there will be others facing similar challenges as you. You may have no idea that a peer is feeling the same way, but understand and please believe that you are not alone."

Dana Harrison

39

Managing Mistakes

We aren't necessarily lost when we go the wrong way

"I believe it is important to establish an atmosphere in the classroom where it is acceptable for students to make mistakes and to acknowledge those mistakes. Mistakes are a window into learning and they should be celebrated, not denigrated. We learn something from every mistake."

-Jim Malone

"When you learn to ride your bike, you can get your first manicure," (one of those things important at the time and now seems silly) I told my youngest, who had asked for years to be able to wear nail polish. Mel responded with a hearty declaration of that we needed to get going. I was still dressed for work as we headed over to the park, and I worried my heels would make it difficult (or impossible) to run behind the bike while holding on. Mel, undeterred, asked for directions, got up on the bike, and took off. So skilled at riding, I had to ask if there had been private practices. But no, Mel was just steady and ready to ride. Mel learning to ride a bike with such ease is the exception to the rule. Whether we know how to ride a bike or not, it begins as an unknown skill to all. Ask most people who have learned, and you'll likely hear stories of the bumps, bruises, and mistakes we suffered along the way. And you'll probably hear riding a bike is now an incorporated skill, unnecessary to learn again.

The fear of making a mistake, particularly when working with kids, is one of the most potent deterrents for adults to avoid engaging in difficult discussions. When asked why they are fearful, caregivers and educators list messing up, ineptitude, and fear of shame, among others. But we have lessons to learn and memories to make.

Unlike riding a bike, learning is not linear. Learning is a wiggly and sometimes circuitous process. We will most certainly have skinned knees at some point before master steering.

Educators and caregivers make over a thousand decisions per day. There is simply no way to avoid mistakes. When I fall into the fear of making mistakes, I try to remind myself that avoiding making a mistake is an energy consumer (see Time and Energy section) and it is an assertion of privilege (not available to all) to be able to avoid situations for fear of making a mistake.

The truth is, we will all mess up. Spending time and energy trying to *avoid* mistakes interferes with learning. The managing mistakes model outlined below was developed to help us move *through* rather than avoid mistake making.

Step 1:

Recognize it as a mistake. As we have good intentions, seeing the error may be difficult in the moment. Find a buddy in your family, friends, and colleagues with whom you have a trusting relationship to alert you when you have made a mistake. As soon as you learn something new, ask, 'How could this knowledge have informed previous experiences? And how *will* it inform future actions?'

Step 2:

Receive feedback about the mistake as a gift. Even though feedback may not feel like a gift, learning from our missteps allows us to be better in the community and grow. Note: Your PLOF is easily activated when we get difficult feedback.

Receiving feedback is not the time to explain or clarify. You might rely on a script (see line please) such as "Thank you, I had not thought of it like that before and will reflect on it. Would it be alright to connect later?"

Step 3:

Realize it is not about you and resist making it about you. This is a necessary and often difficult task. Our intentions are not our impact. When we try to explain away a mistake by talking about our intention—when we respond rather than hear—we are often just shielding ourselves from taking responsibility. It's a normal response, but it risks damaging our relationships with the person offering feedback and/or with the person or people impacted by our mistake. It robs us of an opportunity to learn and get better at what we do.

Nan, horrified with her actions repeated throughout the day her disbelief and upset. Leading a faculty meeting, Nan referred to folders as 'flesh colored' instead of 'manila.' About 20 minutes later, Nan realized her mistake, apologized to the group, and continued her presentation. Nan was visibly flustered during the discussion, and after the meeting, she shared her disappointment with friends reliving her embarrassment. Nan *intended* to make everyone in the faculty workshop feel included. Her *impact*, however, was hurtful, particularly to her colleagues of color, and showed a lack of awareness. She was so focused on her reaction, Nan didn't hear a White colleague say he didn't know what the big deal was which only served to compound the impact of Nan's initial statement. Nan did not talk to her colleagues of color because she worried they would not want her to and that she would say the wrong thing. Nan's reaction focused on herself and her emotional response to the blunder she made. In focusing on herself, she neither took responsibility for the hurt she caused her colleagues of color, nor helped her White colleague understand the hurtful impact of her statement.

Strategies to resist making it about yourself include:

1. Get validation elsewhere! Eliminate statements such as "You know I am a good person, right?"
2. Engage in your learning.
3. Acknowledge there is a gap between our intentions and our impact. Think of

a 90 to 10 ratio and try to spend 10% (or less) of time, energy, and words on my *intentions* and 90% (or more) of time, energy, and words on the *impact*(s) I had on others.

4. Feel the feelings but give them a curfew. I find it deeply troubling when I mess up. But sitting in feelings too long conflicts with learning, so I assign a curfew. I set my alarm for 15 minutes, then spend that time in the emotions and engaging with my PLOF care plan. When the alarm rings, I remind myself shamed brains cannot learn, I have work to do, and I need to focus on my learning.

As always, kids have the best answers, and Miguel, an eleventh-grader, said it best. "Avoid over-apologizing, defending, and rationalizing. None of it is helpful when talking about mistakes. If you hear the words 'I' or 'me' more than you hear apologetic words or questions about how to make it right, you have made it about you."

Step 4:

Reflect on your learning internally and reflect your learning in your actions. Internal reflection helps us learn so that we don't repeat our mistakes. Demonstrating our learning includes shifting our language, listening, and taking steps to repair any relationships we may have harmed. Authentically reflecting on our learning is more than deciding not to say or do a specific thing again. It is examining *why* it should not be said and what lead to the comment being said.

A process I find helpful for reflecting on my mistakes:

- **One** sentence describing the issue.
- **Two** lessons to learn.
- **Three** resources for learning.
- **Four** ways to demonstrate my growth.

Step 5:

Resist learning for rewards. Saviorism (doing *for* others), posturing (masking mistakes, overcompensating), and speaking through or on behalf of others create a perception of credibility. It feels good. Generally speaking, doing for others <u>is</u> a positive, and it lights up the pleasure center of our brain, but this makes saviorism and posturing all the more seductive. And while it might look or feel good, it takes way our chance to *be* better.

Step 6:
Repair the relationship. When accepting an apology, Bergan, a sixth grader, wanted his friend to know trust was fragile by saying, 'If the handle comes off a mug and you use superglue, you can still use it. But if it breaks again or in too many places, you either get cocoa all over you, or you have to throw it away.'

Repairing the harm is all about the person for whom harm has been caused. Nan might have offered 'I realize I caused pain and am deepening my learning' and 'I want to make this right and wonder if you know what you need' while inviting the other person into a collaborative conversation. Being careful not want to put the onus of our growth on the harmed party.)

Step 7:
Resume the normalcy of the relationship by showing you are learning and that you care about the relationship.

After attending a workshop on boundaries, Andre, believing it unnecessary, asked Liz to tell him if his jokes were ever problematic. When Liz shared that some of his jokes pushed her limits, Andre fell silent and went into his office. He avoided hanging out at lunch (as she had in the past) and, for a time, didn't make the typical small talk he and Liz had enjoyed. Andre was processing the feedback and felt embarrassed about his actions. But Liz interpreted his changed behavior as anger and thought she could not be honest with Andre in the future.

Telling someone about a mistake you made takes energy and can make us feel vulnerable. Being told we made a mistake can be embarrassing, but growth takes responsibility for previous actions and monitors our response to the feedback.

After some reflection, Andre reconnected with Liz and took ownership of his unwelcome jokes and behavior upon receiving the (requested) feedback. He also asked Liz what she needed to repair their relationship. It took time, but Andre grew from the process, and he and Liz resumed a healthier working relationship.

Step 8:

A loaded but necessary step in managing our mistakes is **remembering that** *having* **the option to avoid issues because of the fear of messing up is a privilege** and *avoiding* a problem for fear of messing up is an *assertion* of that privilege.

For example, as a heterosexual, (in my case, being a woman attracted to men), I can avoid conversations about sexual orientation. I can also talk freely about my husband without fear of harm, not true for many in the LGBTQIA+ community. If the community is not open and affirming, they might feel forced to code-switch, either changing gender pronouns when they speak about loved ones or avoid speaking altogether for fear of reprisals.

"We need to forgive our mistakes. Even by thinking through what you would say, you have an impact on a future response."

Lauren Brownlee

40

Honor the Power of an Apology

It's never too late to say you are sorry

I was in a professional development workshop that helped me reconsider a situation from years ago. The content of the discussion made me see a mistake with a student. I felt embarrassed but also grateful for the opportunity to gain new insight. A short while later, I saw the student, now graduated, at an alumni event. We spoke. He allowed me to convey my realized mistake and offer an apology. He graciously accepted my apology and reminded me of the importance of continuing my learning journey.

We all step into conversations and situations outside of our experiences, and they can be terrifying. Phrases signaling openness might include:

- This is a new conversation for me, so I may mess it up.
- I am still learning.
- You used a word new to me. Can you tell me what it means to you?

A student once said to me, "I want adults to learn what they need to learn to have conversations with me. But if the choice is talking even if they make a mistake, or not talking at all, I would rather the mistake."

We must be brave. As we learn new information, we may look back and realize we owe someone an apology. It's never too late to tell someone we wish we had handled a situation differently. It can be a compelling moment of shared humanity.

"Freedom is not worth having if it does not include the freedom to make mistakes."

Mahatma Gandhi

Mistake Reflection Activity:

Learning solidifies through multiple modalities of instruction; therefore, this activity requires thinking, writing, and stating.

1. Focus on a mistake. It could be one you have made or one you fear making. Be specific. Name those directly and indirectly impacted. Recall where it was, describing the environment (private space or public place). Think about when it was. Were either of you rushing from one place to another? Was the time scheduled, planned, or spontaneous?
2. Locate and listen to the signals from your physical location of feelings. Consider what you can do to silence your PLOF.
3. Work through the steps:
   a. Recognize the mistake. Answer *how* it was that you came to realize your error and how you reacted.
   b. Receive feedback. Describe in one or two sentences the feedback you received. What was your PLOF saying, and how did you respond? If you were receiving input from another person, what did you say in response to them?
   c. Realize it is not about you. If it were about you, what would you want to have known?
      i. How did you reflect on what you needed to learn?
      ii. How was your learning reflected in your words or actions?
      iii. What next steps do you want to take in your learning?
      iv. What were your intentions and your impact?

   v. Imagine a valley with your intentions on one side and the impact on the other side. How far apart are they?

 d. Reflect. Looking back, what did you learn both at the moment of realization and later on?

 e. Remember privileges.

   i. Is this situation an example of one you can avoid in the future?

   ii. How do your privileges impact your future behaviors concerning this situation?

 f. Pulling it together: If the situation replicated itself, how would your new understanding present? What will you do, say, learn in the future? And what resources, education, experiences do you need?

Tell someone about the situation and what you learned.

"The outcome is non-negotiable, but we will recognize the struggle to get there and will walk the path together as long as you are willing to go there."

Nishant Metha

41

When "I Don't Know" Is the Wisest Response

Admitting we don't know can better our partnership

M r. Zumstein made me, a tenth-grade girl, feel seen and heard by telling me he didn't know what I was feeling but he was here to help.

I was all set to live with my dad so I could go to an accredited high school. (our commune school was phenomenal but not accredited to offer diplomas). But in the end of eighth grade my dad was killed so as a ninth grader, I enrolled in a new public school for the first time in my life (up until that point, I had been homeschooled on The Farm.) I was nervous to walk into this new environment, but my mom helped me prepare.

My mom advised me not to tell anyone at school where I lived. Do my hair a certain way and wear different clothes, so you looked like the other kids in school. And I was confused. Honesty was a core value in our home, so lying to the classmates I was about to meet felt wrong. But the seriousness of my mom's expression told me to follow her instructions perfectly.

'New environment' turned out to be an understatement. It was an alien planet. Everything was so different. Lockers lined the halls; the building was filled with people my age (more than I had ever seen in one space) having conversations on

147

topics I had zero experience with. Even though the academic expectations were new. I was lost. The school even told my parents that if they moved to another country, I would have had an easier time.

But I adapted. And I managed to keep details about my home life and upbringing private. Over time, I heard rumors about The Farm. The assumptions made about my home (rampant drug use, free love, dirty people) were so far from the truth that I would have thought they were referring to an entirely different place. But I knew better. I wanted to defend my family, friends, and home. I didn't. Instead, I now understood why mom advised me not to tell anyone where I lived. I was grateful for the clothes and hair advice. Mom had given me an invisibility cloak, masking who I was and letting me navigate the day un-judged. However, I wasn't fully myself at home or at school. Sitting on the laundry mat roof with Robert and Eddie, eating snacks, and looking at stars was the time I felt authentic because I knew them both at home and school.

One day, new students enrolled at our school. Well, new to them, not to me. they were also from The Farm as well, but unlike me, they did not seek to be invisible. People knew where they were from, and they were upset. *Those kids* were invading *our* school, and *their* presence would harm the community.

In what must have been a well-intentioned idea, an administrator told everyone to calm down, to relax, and that it wasn't nearly as big a deal as they feared it was. That another student from the Farm had attended the school and had done very well. He meant it as a compliment. But all I heard was the floor opening up and the oceans beneath swallowing me whole. It only took a few class periods for the rumors to blossom into confirmation. I was one of *them*. Friends turned their backs. Teachers treated me differently. I was drowning.

But there was Mr. Zumstein, my homeroom teacher telling me he didn't know what it's like or even that he understood. But our homeroom was for me too and he was there. That moment, that feeling of being seen, being accepted, that warmth wrapped itself around me that morning. The warmth faded some as I had to leave homeroom to go to my other classes that I knew I had a place in school to retreat to, if necessary. Mr. Zumstein (we called him Old Zummy, even though I think he was only 35) didn't lie to me. He didn't tell me everything would be OK or try to fix it or tell me of a moment when he felt misunderstood. He listened to me. He heard me. He acknowledged how hard it must be for me without making it about himself. His response communicated, 'I am here, I see you, and I want to help.' And for a while that was enough.

42

It's Not Your Imagination: Kids Are
Different Today

**Development, diversity, athletics, and devices have
changed, as have our relationships with each**

"They didn't have bike paths when I was little," said Jim, a long-time resident, as he took a trip down memory lane. "I wonder what kind of ride the developers thought the kids would take with only 20 feet of the bike path."

The local government where I live requires all new construction to include bike paths along the property. I can't remember when this began, but older properties stand out with uneven yet seamless sidewalks (but no bike paths).

The new properties have bike paths, but the ordinance didn't specify that they had to connect to anything at all. These beautifully constructed areas have bike paths that begin and end randomly, sometimes connecting with another new property and stopping short where an uneven sidewalk begins.

Just like the bike paths, today's social and emotional experience for children is fundamentally different from what it was just 20 years ago. As you read the following pages, please consider your PLOF and know that our HUBs to come will help to bridge with your child or students.

There are four spheres significantly different for kids today from just 20 years ago. These spheres are athletics, devices, development, and diversity.

ATHLETICS

Before discussing athletics, it is important to note many students do not participate in sports for personal reasons. These reasons may include desire, lack of access, interest, resources, confidence, and ability. It's important to be especially attentive to stereotypes of children and sports such as tall Black boys playing basketball.

More than one coach or caregiver has concluded that I am critical of athletic programs when talking about this sphere. I see the benefits with my kids and students, including the physical outlet, learning to work with others, setting goals, increasing serotonin (the chemical associated with happiness), and developing social relationships. I see these benefits deriving from other activities as well, and wish those activities were equally valued by society, (but that's a concern for another book). The focus of this section is our changing relationship with athletics, but it is not meant as an expectation of athletic engagement.

Though sports themselves may not be that different, the relationship to athletics has profoundly changed. Most prominently, athletics have become for many families the primary orientation for their calendar, and for many kids, the primary focus of their identity.

As an example, in 2006, Logan joined a summer swim team. He was six years old. We registered for the team in May, and he swam in June and July; by August, the season was over, and we moved on to the next sport. Over the years, swimming became Logan's primary focus. His team commitments extended beyond the summer team, until, eventually swimming flooded our calendar. By the end of eighth grade, Logan swam before school and after school all year long. And in the summer, he doubled up, swimming also for his summer team. As a parent new to year-round swimming, I asked a veteran parent when the team held the end-of-season parties. Her response clarified that this was a new environment for all of us: "We don't have end-of-season parties. The only way I know the new season has started is when I write another check."

For kids with the aptitude, interest, and financial resources, year-round team sports have advantages. Student athletes have the opportunity to hone their skills and develop deeper relationships with each other and their coaches. Year-round sports teams can also create challenges. The rolling from one season to another may cause avoidance of building the skills associated with starting fresh, getting to know new people, welcoming new teammates, and experiencing a beginning, middle, and end. So common are year-round sports there is often no natural decision point about whether a child (or a family) wants to continue. The full-time, full-year commitment happened slowly and was maintained without any deliberate decision-making.

Mali declared that she was a runner while introducing herself during orientation. Like many young people, Mali saw herself wrapped up in and through her athletics. Her identity was so knitted with her athletics that she considered her academics, hobbies, and friends (not to mention her dreams, goals, culture, or family) like they were an afterthought. Conflating this one part of her identity with her view of herself meant her self-worth was determined by how well she did or did not perform.

Another change is the expectation of athletic competence at younger and younger ages. Our family values our children learning to win well, lose well, and be good teammates; athletic experiences meet these values. In third grade, Mel decided to play softball. We registered, listed some friends for carpool, and attended the softball clinic determining team placement. The coach expressed concern before seeing Mel's ability, because the other players had played for a few seasons. He suggested hiring a private coach to work with Mel and build skills. Mel was eight years old and new to the sport, but was immediately being encouraged to major in it. Many children are encouraged to dedicate themselves to a single sport year-round, often on multiple teams, in early elementary school.

Washington Post writer Michelle Mundey, wrote, "The Worldwide Leader in Prep Basketball Coverage, Coast 2 Coast puts out a watch list for second-graders before rankings start with the third grade." "Jerry Love, the founder of Middle School Elite, starts ranking players in the first grade, declares himself the authority for pre-high school basketball."

Sports are competitive, and competition can be healthy. But when athletic performance becomes all-encompassing or when Mali is and only is a runner, it is not. I wonder what happens when kids reach early adolescence, and their quickly changing bodies may not do the same things. And how do they define themselves if they become injured or lose interest?

This early majoring in sports also has the potential for physical consequences. Dr. James Andrews noted his ability to "put top athletes back together," described to Dennis Manolof of Cleveland.com: "Specialization leads to playing the sport year-round. That means not only an increase in risk factors for traumatic injuries, but a sky-high increase in overuse injuries. Almost half of sports injuries in adolescents stem from overuse."

In addition to identity being impacted by athletic abilities, so too is the body. I was surprised when a mom attending one of my workshops at her child's school invited me to talk with her colleagues in orthopedic surgery. One of the observations they offered was that instead of surgery, many sports-related injuries (particularly overuse injuries) might resolve with physical therapy and time away from the sport. However, when asked to choose between time away from the sport or surgery, many caregivers increasingly select surgery.

Adding to the normalcy is that travel teams have become big businesses. Initially created to allow athletes to compete at a higher level, travel teams have exploded in size and scope, increasing their offerings, availability, and profits. In 2017, *TIME* magazine published "How Kids' Sports Became a $15 Billion Industry," stating, "The U.S. youth-sports economy—everything from travel to private coaching to apps that organize leagues and live stream games—is now a $15.3 billion market." According to the Aspen Institute's Project Play, written in 2020, "travel teams are listed as a prime opportunity for the spread of COVID-19, and yet organizers have a financial incentive to resume sooner rather than later. For many, this is their livelihood. According to *Florida Today*, event cancellations cost USSSA $4.5 million in revenue." Aspen Project Play recognizes the impact on regular team participation as well, stating "travel teams have also impacted a decrease in regular team participation dropping from 45% in 2006 to 37% in 2016." Travel teams, by definition, require time away from home, potentially leaving behind many families with limited financial means or flexibility to travel with their children.

As stated at the start of this section, I am an enthusiastic fan of childhood athletics and offer these statistics not to shame or talk readers out of organized sports. Instead, I advocate for regular check-ins with your child or student about their desires and goals, asking "Is this still working for you?" "Why or why not?"

One of the gifts of our children's athletics is the shared experience with other caregivers. The interests, language, and goals create connections for caregivers, their children, and other caregivers. With the fast pace of our lives, many caregivers find a merging of social life connected and their children's sports. The sidelines become small communities, with conversations picking up at one game and ending at the next game or practice. 'We are going to be the champs!!!' shouted caregivers from the sidelines, their enthusiasm bathing everyone in the excitement. Students regularly express gratitude for caregiver support, but Juan best summarized the interesting disconnect: 'They're so excited when we win, exclaiming 'We won!' But when we lose, I hear messages such as so sorry *you* lost. I celebrate the athlete's hard work, yet I wonder who are the 'we'? My husband and I were caregivers on the same sidelines, and as far as I could see, our contribution to the team's success was driving carpools, providing snacks, and cheering for each player by name.

Lastly, it has always been common for coaches and athletic directors to communicate behavioral guidelines; however, increasingly, the procedures are for the caregivers. "Ref, that is f*&^%& up, the score is wrong!!" shouted a parent from the other team. Our then 16-year-old, Logan kept the scorebook for Mel's fourth-grade softball team and had just told the referee the score he had tallied. Hearing the parent's response, the ref followed the normal process of approaching the other team scorekeeper to confirm they have the exact figures. Both scorekeepers confirmed the same tally for the referee, but instead of appreciation, they were only met with more cussing at an increased volume from the parent, putting our 16-year-old in the position of reminding the parent it was a softball game for fourth graders.

Caregiver and educator tips for detangling identity and athletics to realign sports as *a factor* not a *determinant* of identity:

1. Help children have varied interests.
2. Describe children for their qualities first, followed by their activities.
3. Ensure check-in points to determine if they still desire participation in that sport before "sending the next check."
4. Remind students they are much more complex and valuable than the sport they play.

Conversation prompts for adults and kids:

1. What are all the roles you can name to describe yourself?
2. What do you most and least enjoy about your sport?
3. How would you know if it was time for a change?
4. How would I know if you were ready for a change?
5. How does being a good winner and loser sound?
   a. How does each appear?
   b. What sort of behavior is problematic?

DEVICES

Thirteen-year-old Jamison asked why adults say they don't want us to 'go online so much?' Jamison was just as mystified by the phrase *online* (referring to dial-up) as by her parents' continual requests to limit her time on her phone. Her class-mates agreed, adding even though they are called 'phones' they don't think of their phones as many adults do (a means to call each other). They think of phones, rather, as a means to learn, entertain, and communicate (via videos, typing, emojis, and more). Another student telling me about a conversation with a friend described as talking all night. I asked if he was *talking* verbally or with his thumbs. His response, of 'text' was paired with a look letting me know my question was ridiculous.

The notion of talking on the phone was as ridiculous to him as it would have been if our parents asked us if we were in touch with friends by telephone or by letter. From party lines to individual telephone numbers, means of communication are constantly evolving and growing (the printing press was revolutionary; now fax machines seem antiquated). These leaps forward rewrite the fabric of how our children socialize, engage with each other, and engage with the world. I bought my first cell phone well into adulthood and sent my first text message by hitting "4" twice and then three more times just to say "Hi." (There was no punctuation; I never figured out the punctuation.) Compared to their friends, my kids were late to the party, getting their first touch screen phones in middle school. Their first messages were text, emojis, pictures, and video.

Even before remote learning, schools were also entwining themselves with technology often as a statement of innovation. Early on, around 2012, we became a one-to-one school with each of our students having a computer or tablet to supplement learning. Our counselor and technology director designed digital citizenship courses focusing on behavior. For many kids today, there is no "online" and "offline"; the worlds have converged. So too must our education. As a counselor today we support teachers to include equally lessons on digital and in-person interactions. For example, when working with students to enhance conflict resolution skills, I ask how they would address challenges *in person* and *on a device*. Discussing the different responses appropriate for in person and on a device, communication allows us to focus on the best and most effective strategies for each, as well when one might be called for over the other.

The way we learn new information is equally changed. When we want to learn something about almost any topic, we Google it or watch YouTube. Googling has become a verb synonymous with gathering information. "Mr. SEO" states, "the key to receiving traffic through Google is to gain first page rankings because first page websites get 91.5% of Google traffic." Topics move up to the top via an algorithm connected to the frequency of searches, lending the leading links a perception of credibility. Search engines are increasingly becoming the source of education for kids, thus bypassing adult input.

Jed said he asked his teacher what being pansexual (not limited in the sexual choice concerning biological sex, gender, or gender identity) meant. Jed felt shut down when a teacher told him the question wasn't appropriate. So, he googled it. Another student asked teachers and caregivers to talk about the events in Charlottesville in August 2017. When the student did not get knowledge, he looked it up on YouTube, watching the death of Heather Heyer over and over. Having only the video as his educational resource, he concluded, that standing up for your beliefs could get you killed, contradicting the same teachers and caregivers encouraging him to be an upstander rather than a bystander. While looking it up online provided words in response to his question, it did not allow for context, follow-up questions, or reflection.

Kids repeatedly share that they want us to know of their relationships with devices but want us to do so in ways that work for them. A couple of years ago, I surveyed several hundred students asking what they wanted adults to know about their relationship to technology. Here's some of the feedback:

- 'A lot of times when I'm on my phone, I'm listening, but might be looking things up, such as the definition to a word a teacher used or the band my friend mentioned. I'm not just going on social media.'
- 'I don't understand why my school and parents tell me not to post pictures without permission, but I can see my parent has posted pictures and stories about me without my permission. And if you go on my school's social media, there are a lot of pictures I didn't permit; it just doesn't make sense.'
- 'I do need the rules of not keeping my phone in my room to keep me from being on it too late ... I may not act grateful, but it helps.'
- 'I don't have anyone at my school whom I know is gay, and through my chat group, I don't feel so alone.'
- 'I wish I could tell my teachers and parents that if they do not want me on my phone between classes, at the dinner table, or a stoplight, you shouldn't be on yours walking down the hall, while out to dinner with me, or at a stoplight. ... Stoplights are not cellphone zones, and neither is the dinner table.'

Pre-Google Activity:

When kids ask a question, they are ready for age- and stage-appropriate responses.

1. Imagine a child asking a question that you either:
   a. Do not know the answer to.
   b. Are not prepared to provide a solution.
2. Check-in with your PLOF. Is it trying to move you from safe to stress zones?
3. Assume that either:
   a. You will give a response.
   b. The response will be obtained through an internet search.
4. Answer the following:
   a. What would you like the child to know?
   b. What message would you want them to hear before doing a search?

Develop a script for when you are caught off guard and unprepared with an answer.

43

Physical and Emotional Development

The timelines of adolescent development are beginning earlier and lasting longer

Until 2013, it was believed that the brain's frontal lobe, responsible for impulse control and decision-making, concluded its development by age 18. The National Institutes of Health (NIH) now believe it reaches maturity in the mid to late 20s. And research initiated by Marcia Herman-Giddens and continued by the American Academy of Pediatrics shows the onset of adolescence is dropping by four to five months for each passing decade.

German researchers found that in "1860, the average age of puberty in girls was 16.6 years. In 1920, it was 14.6; in 1950, 13.1; 1980, 12.5; and in 2010, it had dropped to 10.5. The age of onset varies slightly by gender, race, and ethnicity." To emphasize, this is a 6.1 year drop in the age of onset of puberty in girls between 1860 and 2010. One can assume it has dropped further since.

From Teen Health: "The earliest physical change of puberty for girls is usually breast development, which most often begins around 10 or 11 years. But it's perfectly normal to start anytime between the ages of 7 and 15." Deborah Roffman offers 'My readings suggest that the average age onset of menstruation is 12.5 and the first ejaculation is 13.5 years both leveled off at the end 20th century. The onset of secondary sex characteristics continues to drop.' My experience tracks with the research in terms of early onset. As a school counselor in 1993, I had a fifth-grade student who had begun menstruation. Now, fellow counselors state many students have started menstruation even earlier. We don't know definitively why these changes have occurred though there are many theories, there is no definitive cause of the earlier onset of puberty. But we do know earlier and ongoing education from parents and educators is profoundly impactful.

Puberty, as Deb Roffman offers 'is a process of physical changes lasting up to ten years and concluding when the full adult height is reached. In the beginning, the process is not visible with one component being the onset of menstruation or ejaculation but is not inclusive of all physical changes as one goes from a male or female-bodied child to an adult. As puberty occurs earlier, so too are the chemical changes that often precede the physical changes.' These chemical changes in the brain are part of readying the body for its development; signs of chemical changes include mood swings, impatience, and more prominent emotional responses.

These changes in development have not, for the most part, changed communication timelines. Most caregivers don't discuss with their seven- (or eight- or nine-) year-olds about puberty and adolescence. Therefore, many kids start puberty without accurate or adequate information. (Similarly, accurate and honest health curricula, where it exists, also starts much later than age seven.)

Given the relationship with devices, our silence on these matters must seem particularly loud. Such silence contrasts to the acknowledgement of early childhood changes and growth stages often discussed and even celebrated. 'Wow, you lost a tooth!' 'You're almost tall enough to reach the top shelf!' Some of us post on social media these momentous occasions such as riding without training wheels or getting braces. In other words, we may not provide the anticipatory guidance, a process used by pediatricians and other health care providers to inform parents of upcoming changes and how to provide support such as reminding parents of the importance of wearing a helmet when riding a bike. We parents then provide the same anticipatory guidance to our children.

But we aren't celebrating or posting on social media our child's nocturnal emissions (wet dreams) or breast bud growth. **(Nor should we!)** But this shift may mean the physical changes of puberty, especially early onset puberty, may be the first physical changes a child undergoes without guidance, education, or preparation.

Many of the early physical manifestations of puberty are hidden by clothing. Therefore, these changes may not be known to adults unless the child speaks up (which is rare). This absence of information combined with a reluctance to talk about physical maturation can lead to a web of secrecy and shame around essential human development. As with neurological shortcuts, online searches are fact-seeking processes. They often replace information given by caregivers and teachers to be sure the results of these searches are not connected to values.

We can do it differently. What if we conveyed to our students and children that we will support them as they grow from children to teenagers just as they were supported going from babies to children? Typically, infants have a continuous adult presence supporting them through each developmental milestone. While it should take a different format, we can and should do the same during adolescence.

Children will have questions. Some we will feel prepared for and many we will not. But if they can ask a question, they are ready to hear an age- and stage-appropriate answer (see Use One Sentence). As discussed earlier, when questions go unanswered by adults, students will seek them elsewhere, including their devices. The information provided by classmates and the internet—especially the information around puberty and sex—is often devoid of context, comprehensive information, and fundamental values.

Over the years, I have heard many parents say that talking about body changes is uncomfortable. And I get it. Talking to my kids about puberty made me nervous too. But we don't want to see what they would learn if they looked up the answers on their own. I was curious, so I Googled some of the questions I have been asked over the years, such as 'Why does my penis stand up at random times?' or 'What are breast buds?' and 'What does semen smell like?' into a search engine, like your child might. Within a few clicks, I was on some sketchy websites, which I can only imagine being scary and confusing for kids.

Suggestions for caregivers:

1. Inquire with your pediatrician when your child may begin puberty.

2. Look for age-appropriate books on body development.
3. Send consistent messages of support.
4. Provide previews that their bodies and feelings will change, reminding your child frequently that you are a resource.

Suggestions for educators:

First, I recognize that some teachers may not have permission to discuss health concerns with students. If this is true in your school you may want to:

1. Look at the age of initiation of your health curriculum for classroom connections. If no health curriculum exists, inquire if and how your school can meet this need.
2. Talk to the student support staff, such as a counselor or nurse, about supporting students. If your school does not have a counselor or nurse, reach out to other schools for ideas.

Suggestions for Caregivers and Educators together:

1. Develop language to use at home and school.
2. Establish and develop plans for ensuring shared goals.
3. Create communication pathways for the child to privately ask questions or communicate physical changes.
4. Remember who is listening (see Four Stages of Listening).

DIVERSITY

JEDIAB (Justice, Equity, Diversity, Inclusion, Access, and Belonging)

Being in my 50s, I was raised not to talk about diversity, particularly race; therefore, engaging with the fluidity of language is a learned skill for me, and I know I am not alone. As people born in the late '90s and early 2000s were labeled *digital* natives, we might write about the current generation of children as *identity* natives meaning they have familiarity with language that many adults do not. Those born in 2000 and beyond are growing up with language, understanding, and experiences new to many of the adults in their lives. They have words but not necessarily experiences, whereas we adults may have the experiences but lack the words. Before proceeding, let's examine the current understanding of language.

Justice is the process of breaking down the barriers that separate different groups. Justice requires **equity**, which is a state in which everyone gets what they need. Equity is not the same as **equality**, which is when everyone gets the same thing. **Diversity** often refers to the presence of people with differing identities. Diversity is data-driven and numerically answers "How many?" Diversity is necessary but not in place of inclusion. **Inclusion** is when the invitation is explicit and active—it is extending an invitation to those beyond the current group. In its authentic sense, inclusion leads to belonging. In **belonging**, everyone feels welcome and able to show up as their whole and authentic self.

Each of these states exists through **access** or proactively ensuring opportunities are available to all.

A person's authentic experience in belonging to a community is affirmed by whether they can express being sincerely seen, heard, known, valued, and cared for by those in their community.

Camille Simone Edwards

IT'S NOT YOUR IMAGINATION: KIDS ARE DIFFERENT TODAY

Social identifiers are the labels we give ourselves, such as race, gender, sexual orientation, beliefs, and more. Since 2000, we've seen significant changes in our understanding, knowledge, application, and navigation of social identifiers, meaning children today are growing up with a fundamentally different understanding of the world and their place in it.

I reviewed the past 100 years in United States history, plotting when social identifiers had significant movement forward. Expectedly, I found profoundly impactful actions from 1920–2000. However, many spread over the 80 years. Unexpectedly and unlike any other era, from 2000–2020, *almost all* social identifiers were deeply moved, often overlapping each other.

"I would most like you to know that your identity is not a set of boxes to check, once and for all, or even a color-by-number painting. Your identity is a constantly evolving work of art unique to you, and it is stunningly beautiful."

Kiri Harris

The following assumes memory is *fixed* around four or five years of age. Before this age, we have "snapshot" memories, and afterward, we have a movie or sequentially connected memory. Our first memory of the timeline becomes what I call anchor memories. Anchor memories define our worldviews, and all facts afterward either contradict or are validated by our anchor memories. For example, because I lived in a bus from age three to six, my anchor memories are that families live in a converted bus without electricity. Therefore, being in my cousin's homes with electricity and multiple rooms was odd for me.

The following plots the anchor memories kids might have related to the experiences in the world occurring around the same time as their memory became "movie-like."

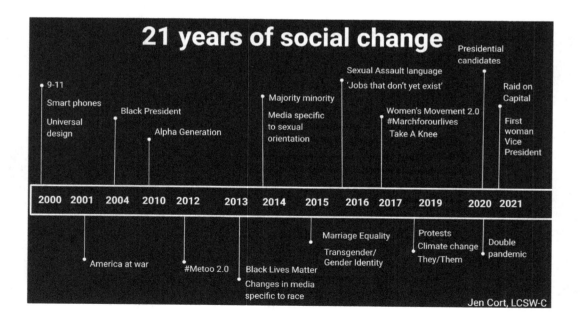

People born in 2000 do not remember life before cell phones or even smartphones. They do not know a world before 9/11.

People born in 2001 have grown up with the United States in a continuous state of war. I once asked a recruiting officer if they thought this impacted their work. They responded that young people today seemed almost casual about war and wholly disconnected from its realities and consequences.

People born in 2004 do not remember a time before having an African American or Black president.

People born in 2010 may not remember a time before the legalization of gay and lesbian marriage.

People born in 2011 do not remember a time before having a White president, former President Trump.

Around this time, the words transgender and gender identity became part of the mainstream lexicon.

People born in 2012 with not remember before the resurgence of the women's movement with #MeToo. They are likely to remember the events commonly referred to as *Charlottesville*, referring to the White nationalist rally in 2017 in opposition to the statue removal of a Confederate general, Robert E. Lee. They will not remember before football star Colin Kaepernick took a knee to protest police violence against Black people, particularly Black men.

People born in 2013 may not remember before racially expansive representations in media when Cheerios made a commercial featuring an interracial family. They will likely not remember before kids stimulated an international climate change movement through social media.

People born in 2014 may not remember before changes in media led to public visibility of LGBTQIA+ families. In 2013, Honey Maid, a graham cracker company, created commercials featuring interracial, gay, and lesbian families eating Honey Maid products. Many advertisers point to the Cheerios and Honey Maid commercials as the beginning of the media embracing all identities.

Our 2014 children are also the first to be born in majority-minority race demographics.

People born in 2015 are part of the Alpha Generation (born in 2010–2025). They are described as highly tech-savvy, the most educated generation of our time, and as people who live in the moment. This generation and the age groups just above them are much more civically engaged, some successfully lobbying states to grant excused absences from school for social and environmental protests.

To learn about trends in younger children, I follow clothing and toy companies. Generating sales and creating long-term brand loyalty (securing their bottom line) depends on understanding what their targeted demographic seeks. Toy and clothing companies put incredible amounts of time, energy, and money into researching current and up-and-coming desires to create the sought-after merchandise. Creators often have focus groups they can listen and learn from. Mattel, the Barbie company, sought to create a doll for the Alpha Generation. When asked what kind of doll they wanted, kids asked for dolls with the options for different gender expressions (changing hair, clothes, accessories, etc.). Mattel developed a Creatable World doll for all genders. These dolls move away from pink/blue, masculine/feminine binary and toward flexibility, individual interests, and (accurate to the name) creativity.

> **Our children are growing up in a new world and with new understandings of that world.**

People born in 2015 will **not remember before what I think of as the *double pandemic*.** One of the pandemics is COVID-19, and the other is discrimination, particularly racial discrimination. Demonstrating how quickly events incorporate into children's practices, I heard from a parent of a kindergartener advocating her children's school to hold mask-free school days. She changed her position when her daughter's stresses became overwhelming at the idea of going to school without a mask because she has no memory of not doing so.

People born in 2016 will not remember a time before the swearing-in of Kamala Harris as the first female and second person of color (Charles Curtis being the first) to the Vice Presidency, or the events of January 6, 2021, insurrection at the United States Capitol.

People born in 2016 will have few, if any, memories before people wore masks. Our children are growing up in a new world and with new understandings of that world. Over and over again, I find that young people do not understand how older people are more recent to these conversations. We may risk reacting with silence, frequently interpreted as lack of care or interest rather than lack of information and comfort. A relatively simple step is for adults to signal the newness of language and understanding (see Can We Take That Again? section).

44

Kids Can Change the World

Helping kids see themselves as change agents

The phrase "preparing our children for the jobs that don't exist yet," became popular during the 2016 election cycle, causing many educators to question how we can do so if we don't know those jobs or the skills needed to do them. But we can tap into the research of Harvard University, *Bloomberg Businessweek*, and other organizations to create a window into these yet-to-exist jobs. Harvard's research led to creating the "Making Caring Common Project" focusing on "raising kids who care about others and the common good." In the 2014 article, "Preparing for Jobs that Don't Yet Exist," Futurist Thomas Frey wrote a list of "Hot New Skills" including:

1. Transitionists: Those who can help make a transition.
2. Expansionists: Adapting along with a growing environment.
3. Maximizers: Maximizing processes, situations, and opportunities.
4. Optimizers: Tweaking variables until it produces better results.
5. Inflections: Finding critical inflection points in a system.
6. Dismantlers – Every industry will eventually end, and this requires talented people who know how to scale things back in an orderly fashion.
7. Feedback Loopers: Those who can devise the best possible feedback loops (systems of providing insights).

8. Backlashers: Ever-new technology will have its detractors, and each backlash will require a response.
9. Last Milers: Technologies commonly reach a point of diminishing returns as they attempt to extend their total capacity to the end user. People with the ability to mastermind these solutions will be in hot demand.
10. Contextualists: In between the application and the big picture lays the operational context for every new technology.
11. Ethicists: People who can ask tough questions and standards to apply moral decency to staggeringly complex situations.
12. Philosophers: With companies in a constant battle over "my-brain-is-bigger-than-your-brain," it becomes the overarching philosophy that wins the day.
13. Theorists: Every new product, service, and industry begins with a theory.
14. Legacies: Those who are passionate and skilled with leaving a legacy.

Frey's list of new careers is fascinating and forward-thinking. Add to that the unique cultural and generation experiences of those born after 2000, and we begin to align our goalposts in this Era of Co-construction.

Throughout the extensive research mentioned above, we see consistent threads of empathy, listening for learning, working together to solve problems previously unseen, and a growing understanding that differences are additives, not dividers. In this way, we adults can learn from and with our children, who may have more comfort with language and more understanding through their unique experiences.

"You are starting to find your voices, which makes you the perfect champions and change agents for diversity and inclusion initiatives in your spheres of influence (your schools, teams, families, churches, and communities). If we provide student leaders with fundamentals, create a safe environment for them to express themselves, and get out of their way, amazing things can happen!"

Alkia B. Jones

Letter to Middle Schoolers

We are entering what I think of as the Era of Co-construction, the era for care-givers and teachers to create goals and guides while working with kids to craft common ethos of families and schools. Education used to look like a single adult standing in the front of the room pouring information into students, referred to as the "sage on the stage." Now educational pedagogy has moved toward adults being the guide on the side through project-based learning, group work, and the understanding that the key to all twenty-first century living is empathy, talking across differences, listening for education, and problem-solving.

Though these paradigms are different for kids to today, young people have always been change agents impacting their communities and the greater world. Continuing this important history, we can look at the Era of Co-construction together, adopting new strategies for navigating conversations with children, even when a topic challenges adults. The period of co-construction means students and adults work together and create the home and classroom ethos and culture. Co-construction does not mean the kids are making all of the decisions, but that kids and adults listen to and consider each other's opinions and insights.

> **Belonging invites us show up as our authentic self, feeling the space is informed by you.**

"In my 48 years of living, I have had eight different jobs, and until I became a police officer, I did not realize that every job along the way prepared me for the duties I perform daily. Life's journeys are many, all leading to one point."

Pet Speight

My work centers on equity (everyone gets what they need), diversity (the differences between people), justice (breaking down barriers between groups), and inclusion (inviting everyone in). As I think about inclusion, an open and available invitation, my mind also goes to belonging. Inclusion is far from the same as belonging. Belonging invites us to show up as our fully and authentic self, knowing the space is informed by your presence. Seeking belonging is the foundation of co-construction; it creates areas where adults and children learn from and with each other.

"I am because we are." *We depend on connection, community, and caring. We are all connected. We cannot be ourselves without community; health and faith are always lived out among others; an individual's well-being is caught up in the well-being of others.*

Ubuntu belief introduced to me by Lauren Brownlee

Artwork by Nate Austin

"I didn't learn anything"

When I first heard this statement, my PLOF was wide awake and ready to protect. No one wants to hear 'No offense, but I didn't learn anything from your workshop.' First, any sentence beginning with 'no offense" will most assuredly be offensive. But the man who waited in line to tell me he learned nothing, went on to say, 'I came into this meeting thinking about all I had to do afterward and hoping you didn't make me feel inept. But I now realize I am not inept. I have been doing good work. I need to refine and continue to learn.' He reflected change happens in both giving new ideas and validating existing ones.

As a belayer (the person holding the ropes while climbers ascend), I have advised students that when they thought they reached their top to straighten their bent leg and reach just one hand higher. When a topic is weighty or challenging, I often ask workshop attendees to look for one thing they will take away, the one thing they will say, think, or do differently—for the one stone to skip. As a systems therapist, I know that systemic and sustainable change happens through one tiny shift at a time. It reminds me of rock climbing.

Just as the bottom of the pond changes with the presence of one stone, I have three hopes for readers:

1. End with one thing you will do differently.
2. Ride along with your PLOF ever-present but not deciding for you.
3. Be an "Old Zummy," acknowledging that you don't know but you care and are present.

Glossary

The following list of terms is a blended document from many resources, including students.

Ability	Often referred to as "mobility," it refers to how we move around in our environment.
Race	Is **not** a biological concept. It defines groups of human beings based on genetically transmitted characteristics (i.e., physical characteristics, including color). The concept of race as used socio-politically by the U.S. Census Bureau reflects self-identification by people according to the race or races with which they most closely identify.
Age	The chronological measurement of years or demarcation by generation.
Ethnicity	Cultural factors, including nationality, regional culture, ancestry, and language.
Religion	An organized system of beliefs, ceremonies, or practices.
Mental Health	A state of well-being in which every individual realizes one's own potential, can cope with the normal stresses of life, can work productively and fruitfully, and is able to contribute to their community.

Neurological Ability	The ability to learn in the manner taught by most teachers requiring few necessary adjustments. There is a range within neurological ability from requiring extensive accommodations to not needing any.
Personality	Individual differences in characteristic patterns of thinking, feeling, and behaving. The study of personality focuses on two broad areas: One is understanding individual differences, in particular personality characteristics, such as sociability or irritability. The other is understanding how the various parts of a person come together as a whole.
Social Ability	How well one is liked and routinely invited or included.
Education	The wealth of knowledge acquired by an individual after studying subject matters or experiencing life lessons that provide an understanding of something. Education requires instruction from an individual or composed literature. The most common forms of education result from years of schooling that incorporates studies of a variety of subjects.
Body Size	The size and shape of one's physical appearance often thought of in relation to gender and age.
Socioeconomic Status	Socioeconomic status is the social standing or class of an individual or group. It is often measured as a combination of education, income, and occupation. Examinations of socioeconomic status often reveal inequities in access to resources, plus issues related to privilege, power, and control.

Gender	One's innermost concept of self as male, female, a blend of both or neither. How individuals perceive themselves and what they call themselves. One's gender identity can be the same or different from their sex assigned at birth.
Sexual Orientation	Sexual orientation is about who you're attracted to and who you feel drawn to romantically, emotionally, and sexually.
Family Constellation	Family constellation is the term coined by Adler and elaborated by Dreikurs to represent the operation of the family system, including caregivers, siblings, and others in the family of origin, together with any others living with them as members of the person's childhood household.
Beliefs	Traditionally related to political and religious spheres; political beliefs are the constructs of ideas that are central to our self-definition.

Part Four

Advices

Advice to caregivers for transitioning to middle school

When I was middle school principal, caregivers often asked "what do kids need to prepare for middle school?" In addition to the academic preparation obtained in elementary school, caregivers can do a few helpful things to get their kids ready for middle school.

1. Learn to use combination locks and learn to open them quickly! Unlike most elementary schools, middle schools (typically) have combination locks on lockers in the hall and locker room. Quickly opening locks allows kids to get the suitable materials for class, avoids the embarrassment of going to the office for help, and provides extra time to check in with friends between classes.

2. Pack all the necessary items for all activities before you leave for school and school for home. As caregivers, we are often helping our kids remember what is needed for sports, camp, and other activities. Teaching your children to pack everything they need for these activities prepares them to bring everything to each class and have everything they need to do their homework at night.

3. Practice starting conversations with people they either don't know well or don't know at all. In elementary school, most kids are with their classmates all day and may have been with some of them for many years. They don't have to practice the skill of making a new acquaintance. In middle school students switch from group to group in classes, lunch, and activities. Knowing how to make a connection helps the day go better and builds new friendships.

4. Learn to do laundry. Yes, doing laundry helps with the middle school transition. So much happens to the growing changing body in these years, and knowing how to do laundry allows children privacy, plus it teaches responsibility and helps caregivers!

5. Develop healthy sleep patterns. Try having your child go to bed and wake up as close to the same time as possible each day. Teens need an average of 9 1/2 hours of sleep a night, and contrary to popular belief, sleeping a great deal on the weekend does not "make up" for that missed sleep during the week.

6. Create code words for uncomfortable social situations. These code words allow kids to 'save face' and avoid other kids becoming upset with them (one of the strongest barriers to asking adults for help.)

7. Develop device-free zones and times. Create spaces and times when family members use no devices. One of our zones is the kitchen table, allowing us time to check in with each other and talk about the day's events. I asked several hundred students what they wanted adults to know about devices. Among their tips was, "I wish when my parents would not bug me about using my phone while they use theirs all of the time." One student added, "when my mom and I go out to dinner, and she's on her phone, it makes me feel like she doesn't want to spend time with me."

8. Help to reduce anxiety by creating a Middle School Bias-free Zone. Students shared with me that they regularly hear adults say, "Ugh, middle school was sooo hard," "Middle school girls are so mean," "Drama!" and more. Such comments may be well-intentioned (or post-traumatic), but they make students feel even more anxious about starting their own middle school experience.

> **Middle school is not a time for caregivers to move out of their child's daily life. However, it is time to find new communication pathways that work for both you and your child, pathways that have the flexibility to adjust as needed.**

Finally, I encourage caregivers to dismiss the stereotype encouraging you to back off or 'let kids go.' Middle school is not a time for caregivers to move out of their child's daily life. However, it is time to find new communication pathways that work for both you and your child, pathways that have the flexibility to adjust as needed.

Advices From Kids

Many of the quotes are sprinkled throughout the book, below is a compilation of advice received from kids.

Dear caregivers,

When complex events are reported at school or in the news, the understandable reaction from adults is to shield our children. But even if we aren't talking about world events at the dinner table, trust that our children hear about them – from their friends, in class, or on social media. So how do we approach these difficult conversations? I surveyed students in many schools and met with St. Paul's School for Girls and Alexander Dawson Mountain School.

Communication:

- Talk about big topics regularly, not just when an issue arises, or you get a letter from the school.
- Set up a time to talk so we aren't taken off guard.
- Give an option for us to speak or not 'when you can.'
- Don't force the topic, but also don't let us opt out of hard conversations.
- Avoid lecturing.
- Speak with us rather than *at* us.
- Share rather than impose your opinion.
- Ask questions about our thoughts and listen for the answers.
- Let us know you are open to listening to us.
- Assure us we won't be in trouble if we have different views than you.
- Know that if you overreact, we won't feel we can share with you, especially after a bad day.
- Tell us you know things are not the same as when you were our age.

- Ask us how you and I can talk about complex topics in the future.

Diversity

- Expose us to your ideas and thoughts.
- Ask questions such as "What does diversity mean to you?"
- Understand prejudice comes from not understanding and know we want to understand.
- Don't shelter us from knowing things; it leads to prejudice and stereotypes because we'll learn everything from the media, friends, and rumors.
- Don't impose your views on us.
- Help us avoid a "loyalty conflict" by not being overly opposed to what we learn at school.
- Know that respecting your opinion does not mean we have to share that opinion.
- Expect us to have a lack of judgment.
- Trust that we can teach you too.

Parenting

- Trust us.
- Give us space. We are finding our true selves, and if we aren't who you think or expect us to be, don't judge us. Assume we are discovering.
- Don't assume our friends are our primary influence on who we will become. We are learning by watching adults too.
- Know we need support to help us discover who we are so we can have a strong belief system supported by caregivers even if it is different than what you want us to be.
- Understand we know we need to do our part to develop our relationships with you.
- Believe we know you want the best for us, and we are often surprised by how we are changing, so don't freak out.

Technology

- "A lot of times when I'm on my phone, I'm listening, but might be looking things up, such as the definition to a word a teacher used or the band my friend mentioned. I'm not just going on social media."

- "I don't understand why my school and parents tell me not to post pictures without permission, but I can see my parent has posted pictures and stories about me without my permission. And if you go on my school's social media, there are a lot of pictures I didn't permit; it just doesn't make sense."
- "I do need the rules of not keeping my phone in my room to keep me from being on it too late … I may not act grateful, but it helps."
- "I don't have anyone at my school whom I know is gay, and through my chat group, I don't feel so alone."
- "I wish I could tell my teachers and parents' If you don't want me on my phone between classes, at the dinner table, or a stoplight, you shouldn't be on yours walking down the hall, while out to dinner with me, or at a stoplight'"… "Stoplights are not cellphone zones, and neither is the dinner table."

Advice from educators, counselors, and more to middle schoolers

Dear Middle Schooler

Quotes sprinkled throughout the book and compiled here in a letter to middle schoolers.

Dear Middle Schooler,

As a counselor, mom, principal, and human, I celebrate you. Your creativity, intelligence, and absolute authenticity amaze me. You are at a decisive age; this is the time you are entirely in charge of deciding who you are going to be! Over time, I hope your peers know how impactful and essential you are to each other and your world. I also know sometimes your age can feel lonely, and it can be easy to believe that you are powerless — despite counselors, principals, advocates, and other people believing in you. I hope you will find our advice helpful.

- "It's okay to do what feels right for you, even if it's not what people seem to want or expect from you. It is valuable to be curious about the experiences and perspectives of others. Still, you are the only one who gets to decide who you are and what is important to you." -Emily Berry, Counselor for Teens and Adults.

- "I wish you all of the courage that you can muster. You'll need it greatly. I hope you realize that because of how your age, race, and gender intersect, adults and peers expect you to think, act, perform, and behave in certain ways that can silence, stifle, and harm the amazing facets dwelling within from shining. You have probably experienced this already. Your job is to work with your friends, find the courage, and maneuver around these labels. And constantly try to shake off the negative expectations that hold you and others back from realizing your extraordinary potential." — Dr. Roderick L. Carey is a Postdoctoral Research Fellow at the Center for Urban Education at the University of Pittsburgh's School of Education.

- "Nobody is the same, and nobody is like you. What I want students to know most about creativity is that you are the representation of it. You are the example of creative energy inside you that comes out in your speech, your clothing, the way you style your hair, the books you read, and with the people you engage. Never let anyone stifle your creativity, and never let anyone tell you that you are no different. Different is what makes you, You." -Ashlee McKinnon, Dance Educator at Capital City Public Charter School.

- Have hope. "What I most hope you know is that people will throw walls up at you at every turn. If you are part of the wall, then your voice for change can weaken the foundation, and over time, the wall will fall. If you are outside the wall, your voice for change can poke holes in the wall and, with strength from others, can blow a gaping hole through which a path can emerge. I hope you build paths between people, question the walls built, and work toward understanding those who are pathfinders and those who are wall builders. By 'seeking first to understand, then be understood' (Stephen Covey), you will be a catalyst for positive change in our world."- Wilson Felter, Head of Middle School Penn Charter.

- "You are starting to find your voices, which makes you the perfect champions and change agents for diversity and inclusion initiatives in your spheres of influence (your schools, teams, families, churches, and communities). If we provide student leaders with fundamentals, create a safe environment for them to express themselves, and get out of their way, amazing things can happen!" -Alkia B. Jones Diversity and Inclusion champion in corporate and academic settings.

- "I would most like you to know that your identity is not a set of boxes to check, once and for all, or even a color-by-number painting. Your identity is a constantly evolving work of art unique to you, and it is stunningly beautiful." Kiri Harris, Middle School Dean Greene Street Friends School.

- "Oscar Wilde famously said, "Be yourself; everybody else is already taken." If you want to contribute to the beautiful diversity of the world, don't bother copying anybody else. You can bring something unique to the world only by bringing the person you're supposed to be!"–Peter Braverman, Founder Arc Professional Development and Former Middle School Head

- "I hope you know you have the power to decide who you will be." Despite the messages you may get from the media you consume or even the people in your life. This decision should be an active, intentional decision, and it should be yours. This decision should celebrate your uniqueness which will unify people in ways many adults have been unable to do. Be willing to make mistakes and be open to learning from them. Insist you are heard. Be ready to ask for help and to offer support to others. Most of all, be you; there is no one better anywhere than precisely who you are! — Jen Cort, Jen Cort Consulting.

Dedication

This book is dedicated firstly to my parents, Carol Taft and Bob Cox, lost too young. When a guest on my podcast, mom shared, *I want people to remember we cannot be complacent, we can be kind, but we need to remember there is work to be done.* My dad, among other things, was a professor to those who are incarcerated and imbued in me *if you have a voice, then speak up, and if you have the ability, do it.* These messages are like threads stitched into everything I do.

Nestled in my heart is my extended family. Along with my parents are my stepparents (so much more than the title affords), James, Dan, and Elaine. My grandmothers, Grace, head-to-toe inspirational and June, the model of what a grandmother should be and one of my best friends. Gratitude to my cousins, whom a friend defines as 'lifelong friends,' Harper, John, Julie, Laurie, and Lisa.

A big, bold, and boisterous gratitude to our sib squad or the fab five–Michelle, Sam, Andrew, and Charlie–for being my co-conspirators on the adventure called life. Special thanks to the sib squad for ensuring one of my favorite roles as auntie to Gus, Adrianna, Olivia, Margo, Halia, Ever, Niko, and Elouise; and sister-in-law to Steve Allen, Alex, and Meredith.

More than any other aspect of my life, my career, this book, my very core, is informed by my beloved Cort family, George, Logan, and Mel. George supports every leap I always make with the belief that I will land on my feet while also holding a net nearby, just in case. Logan and Mel who inspire me to be more, to do more, and grow. I walk through the world enveloped by the joys that you chose me to be your mom and that I get to see your impact on the world.

It's impossible to overemphasize the support of my friends who have become family. I love you dearly, thank you for the walks, talks, silence, hugs, space, laughter, and tears.

HELP US BEGIN

Special thank you to my professional village, the stupendous Saturday writing team, the magical master mind women, and consultants sharing space. Deep gratitude to Andrew Geha for the excellent editorial care and Nate Austin for bringing PLOF to life.

When I took the leap of turning down a head of school position and deciding to go out on my own, I wondered if it was the best decision, but I benefited from the support and wisdom of many. Holding up a few folks who particularly supported me as I developed a career from broken pieces- Kaytura Felix, Randolph Carter, Penny Evins, Johnnie Foreman, Brenda Crawley, Karen Cumberbatch, Montana Wilson, Lauren Brownlee, Brooke Carroll, Alecia Berman-Dry (and AIMS), and the communities of Friends Council of Education, Pennsylvania Association for Middle Level Education, Association for Middle Level Education, and National Small Schools.

This book would have happened without the Association of Middle Level Educators, the editing team, and most of all Paul Meck for introducing us and Stephanie Simpson for believing in my voice. I offer deep appreciation to the schools, students, parents, caregivers, faculty, staff, trustees, and more, who invite me into their most precious communities. I am deeply grateful for my guests on Third Space With Jen Cort, offering real-time professional development to listeners and me. It is a privilege to work with phenomenal people, and I thank you for bringing me into your communities.